# A FREE AND HARDY LIFE

Library of Congress Control Number
2011926842
ISBN-13 978-0-9825597-8-9

Distributed by The University of Oklahoma Press
Designed by Image Printing, Inc.   imageprinting.com
Printed in Canada
10 9 8 7 6 5 4 3 2 1

Cover images (front) President in doorway of West Divide Creek
ranch house, with "Skip" on his lap. Courtesy Library of Congress.
(back) Theodore Roosevelt rides in a Santa Fe railroad engine, before
reaching Redlands, California. Courtesy of a cooperative effort
between the Library of Congress and the Theodore Roosevelt Center
at Dickinson State University.

The Dakota Institute Press
of the Lewis & Clark Foundation
2576 8th Street Southwest, Post Office Box 607
Washburn, North Dakota 58577
www.fortmandan.com
1.877.462.8535

# A Free and Hardy Life:

*Theodore Roosevelt's Sojourn in the American West*

by Clay S. Jenkinson

Foreword by Douglas Brinkley

To Catherine Missouri Walker Jenkinson

the light of *my* life


and


To Sheila Schafer

always the youngest person in every room

# PREFACE

This book was made possible by two remarkable developments in Theodore Roosevelt's Dakota badlands. Medora is the portal village for Theodore Roosevelt National Park (established 1947). Founded in 1884 by the French aristocrat and cattle baron the Marquis de Mores, Medora had become a shabby but delightful near-ghost town by the beginning of the twentieth century. It was restored in the 1960s and 70s by North Dakota entrepreneur and philanthropist Harold Schafer, to whose widow, my friend Sheila Schafer, this book is dedicated. Schafer restored the old Rough Riders Hotel that was built in Medora in 1884, using some of the hotel's original lumber. In 2008, the Theodore Roosevelt Medora Foundation undertook an ambitious remodeling, rebuilding, and expansion of the hotel. The foundation asked me to create a 23 by 27 inch interpretive panel for each of the 70 rooms of the new Rough Riders Hotel, most of them about Roosevelt's time in the American West, especially Dakota Territory, but also about the man and leader Roosevelt became in the West. Those panels served as the basis of this book. They are reproduced with minor variations on the right hand pages of *A Free and Hardy Life.* You will find a small amount of repetition in the historical vignettes, inevitable, given the assignment of providing a different panel for each room, but with no guarantee that any hotel visitor would ever see more than few of the panels.

Beginning in 2005, Dickinson State University, just a handful of miles east of Roosevelt's beloved badlands, launched a series of Theodore Roosevelt initiatives—annual humanities symposia, publications, exhibits, signage, and other interpretive activities. The centerpiece of DSU's initiative is an audacious project to digitize the papers of the 26th President of the United States. The Roosevelt Center's formal partners include the Library of Congress, Harvard University, and the National Park Service. Endorsed by the Theodore Roosevelt Association, the Roosevelt Center has already digitized approximately 750,000 pages of Roosevelt's papers, including letters, photographs, film footage, cartoons, diaries, newspaper clippings, scrapbooks, audio recordings, and more. The Roosevelt Center's mission is to become the most comprehensive Roosevelt archive in the world, to become—effectively—a national virtual Theodore Roosevelt Presidential Library.

Most of the photographs that grace this book were drawn from the extensive and growing archives of the Theodore Roosevelt Center in Dickinson. So were the documents that are reproduced in the Introduction.

The Theodore Roosevelt Center is located on the campus of Dickinson State University, 35 miles east of the Little Missouri River Valley where Roosevelt lived and worked between 1883 and 1887. The Roosevelt Center's plans include the comprehensive archive of the Roosevelt papers, a museum, a reading room furnished in red leather and stout wood, a traditional primary and secondary Roosevelt library, and a convening center.

For more information, please consult www.theodorerooseveltcenter.org and www.medora.com.

*Clay Jenkinson*

It was still the Wild West in those days, the Far West, the West of Owen Wister's stories and Frederic Remington's drawings, the West of the Indian and the buffalo-hunter, the soldier and the cow-puncher. That land of the West has gone now, 'gone, gone with lost Atlantis,' gone to the isle of ghosts and of strange dead memories. It was a land of vast silent spaces, of lonely rivers, and of plains where the wild game stared at the passing horseman. It was a land of scattered ranches, of herds of long-horned cattle, and of reckless riders who unmoved looked in the eyes of life or of death. In that land we led a free and hardy life, with horse and rifle. We worked under the scorching midsummer sun, when the wide plains shimmered and wavered in the heat; and we knew the freezing misery of riding night guard round the cattle in the late fall round-up. In the soft springtime the stars were glorious in our eyes each night before we fell asleep; and in the winter we rode through blinding blizzards, when the driven snow-dust burnt our faces. There were monotonous days, as we guided the trail cattle or the beef herds, hour after hour, at the slowest of walks; and minutes or hours teeming with excitement as we stopped stampedes or swam the herds across rivers treacherous with quicksands or brimmed with running ice. We knew toil and hardship and hunger and thirst; and we saw men die violent deaths as they worked among the horses and cattle, or fought in evil feuds with one another; but we felt the beat of hardy life in our veins, and ours was the glory of work and the joy of living."

*Autobiography*
"In Cowboy Land"

# FOREWORD

## By Douglas Brinkley

Sculptor Gutzon Borglum believed that the United States' ascent to greatness would be known as the "Colossal Age" in history. Everything in America was Paul Bunyan big: the forests, mountains, deserts, lakes, rivers, bridges, factories, farms, and skyscrapers. What concerned Borglum, however, was that there wasn't a proper monument in America bigger than a "snuff box." Full of hubristic determination Borglum—a St. Charles, Idaho, native—decided to carve a vast entablature in the Black Hills of South Dakota honoring the most indispensable of statesmen. His direct aim was to make an American sphinx for the ages with the faces of the leaders most responsible for the United States' "creation and preservation." Dynamite would be needed to blast away rock on Rushmore from the outset before the chiseling could commence on what President Franklin D. Roosevelt called the "shrine of democracy."

The idea of the Mount Rushmore project is credited to South Dakota state historian Doane Robinson. He brought the idea to Borglum who had instituted a similar public arts project on Stone Mountain, Georgia, of various Confederate leaders. A burning question of the late 1920s was what visages belonged on Mount Rushmore. Once Borglum declared he wanted four faces the matter became open to public debate. Washington was an obvious choice; after all he had been the dominant figure of the American Revolution, the Constitutional Convention, and the establishment of the U.S. government. Jefferson was another strong candidate. Besides being author of the Declaration of Independence, he had doubled the size of the United States with the Louisiana Purchase of 1803. Abraham Lincoln, considered the greatest of all presidents for preserving the Union, was a no-brainer. Everybody boosted his inclusion. This left wide open the fourth face slot. Conjecture was rampant. Borglum, however, had a clear-eyed vision—Theodore Roosevelt, his personal hero, whom he called "preeminently an all-American President." He wanted that face blasted onto his South Dakota mountainside.

Roosevelt had died in 1919 but he probably would have shouted "Bully!" at Borglum's rationale for including him on Mount Rushmore. One of my friends who works for the National Park Service at Mount Rushmore told me recently that among the most commonly asked questions from tourists to the National Monument is still, "Why was Roosevelt chosen to be carved on Mount Rushmore?" To some Roosevelt seemed like the odd man out on the mountainside. The short answer to that question is that Borglum thought T.R. belonged on the Black Hills rock because of his seminal role in celebrating America's Manifest Destiny in his book *The Winning of the West*. Then there was Roosevelt's outdoors ethos. From 1901 to 1909, in fact, Roosevelt had saved 234 million acres of Wild America via a series of revolutionary conservation programs. Roosevelt had also built the U.S. Navy into being a great fleet and ordered the construction of the Panama Canal. In a 1924 speech to the Rapid City Lion's Club, the feisty Borglum announced his resolute intention to make T.R. the fourth face.

A lot of fools back in the 1920s challenged Borglum's inclusion of Roosevelt on Mount Rushmore. The old sculptor brushed them aside like gnats. How could T.R. *not* be included? (A contingent was lobbying for Lewis and Clark, John Fremont, Jim Bridger and other characters from the annals of Westward expansion). Wasn't he the president who changed the name of the Executive Mansion to the White House? By building the Panama Canal alone, Borglum argued, Roosevelt "completed the dream of Columbus, opened the way to the East, joined the waters of the great East and West seas." Nobody, Borglum insisted, represented "continental expression" quite like Roosevelt. (And Lewis and Clark were, in a sense, covered by Jefferson's inclusion.)

What a pity that Borglum didn't have Clay Jenkinson's marvelous *A Free and Hardy Life: Theodore Roosevelt's Sojourn in the American West* to hand out to to those citizens pulling for James Madison or Woodrow Wilson or James K. Polk to be carved in the Rushmore memorial. Using a combination of photographs, quotations, historical reasoning, wild facts, and old-fashioned chronology, Jenkinson ably argues the merits of Roosevelt's multi-faceted career in these pages just as Borglum did in the 1920s. In a sense Jenkinson's entire book is a clear-headed rationale for Roosevelt's inclusion as the fourth face on the Shrine of Democracy. It's a pro-T.R. historian's brief. A lot of interesting biographical factoids are illuminated here. As Jenkinson, the Roosevelt scholar-in-residence at Dickinson State University, makes vividly clear, Roosevelt was an explorer, naturalist, war hero, writer, biographer, rancher, and statesman. He wore so many hats that his appeal was kaleidoscopic. Roosevelt, for example, is the only Rushmore-carved president who actually explored both Dakotas (North and South). The badlands were the ecosystem that fulfilled T.R.'s need for romance and self-reliance like none other. Between 1883 and 1887 he operated two ranches along the Little Missouri River embracing the "strenuous life" of the Great Plains as if it were a cure. The village of Medora, North Dakota—gateway to Theodore Roosevelt National Park—was Roosevelt's favorite place on the planet (with the possible exception of Oyster Bay, New York). In a Dickinson, North Dakota, speech on July 4, 1886, Roosevelt declared: "I am, myself, at heart, as much a Westerner as an Easterner. I am proud, indeed, to be considered one of yourselves."

History is hard to know because of all the hired bunk and conspiracy theories that poison the bloodstream of our past. But it isn't hard to understand why Roosevelt belongs on the mountainside. Consider Jenkinson's book a colorful endorsement of Borglum's decision. He has promoted the Roosevelt legacy with fine literary flourishes throughout. The book—like Roosevelt himself—isn't sedate. It serves as a fine primer of remembrance, a wake-up call to cherish our beloved Rough Rider turned Trust Buster, a rustic leader moving America on horseback into the Age of the Model T. All of Roosevelt's public service accomplishments are grappled with here. Yet, this book serves as far more than an Interstate 94 curio-shop souvenir or Medora coffee table gift. For Jenkinson has done a protean job of chaffing the wheat of Roosevelt's life, serving it up to us fresh like homemade bread. It's a high-quality work. I read it with utter *dee-light*... you will too. As Jenkinson—a brilliant scholar and good friend—undoubtedly knows, taking a ride with Teddy is never dull; he was neon before the word was even entered into the dictionary.

The founding ceremony dedicating the figure of Theodore Roosevelt on Mount Rushmore occurred on July 2, 1939 (just as war was erupting in Europe). Hitler and Stalin, in fact, were poised to sign a "Non-Aggression Pact" and poor Poland was about to learn what *blitzkrieg* meant. The T.R. unveiling was held on a Sunday night with over 12,000 people in attendance. By twilight the day rain had passed. The western sky was a vast polar blue filled with burgeoning stars. You could smell the cool stone and fresh pine. The anticipation was great. At nightfall Roosevelt's face was suddenly unveiled, illuminated with firework-like flares.

Everybody roared approval. The audience then took part in a sing-along of Irving Berlin's brand new anthem "God Bless America," the chorus sung with full-throated glee by all the attendees. A near full moon made the whole Black Hills scene that July feel like a religious revival evening. Somehow Borglum had drilled a perfect set of spectacles on Roosevelt's wide face. When it came to oration, Borglum, instead of laundry-listing Roosevelt's public accomplishments, turned the podium into a bully pulpit. He lectured about the gathering war clouds in Europe. "We are at the spearhead of a mighty World movement—an awakened face in rebellion against the worn and useless thought of yesterday," Borglum intoned. "We are reaching deep into the soul of mankind, and through democracy building better than has ever been built before."

Those weren't what Roosevelt called "weasel words." Borglum wanted to make sure the fighting spirit of Rooseveltian Democracy was heard that July night in honor of America's 26th president. Somewhere over the western range, Roosevelt, the cowboy president, Borglum believed, must have been smiling broadly on that moon-washed American night in the Black Hills of Dakota. Hopefully the readers of this handsomely illustrated book will find the same patriotic spirit of Roosevelt bursting forth from these well-written pages. I certainly did.

Douglas Brinkley

Author of *The Wilderness Warrior: Theodore Roosevelt and the Crusade for America.*

# INTRODUCTION:
## *A Soul as Big as the West*

When Theodore Roosevelt visited Medora, North Dakota, briefly on a campaign swing through the American West in 1900, he said, "It is here the romance of my life began." [1] When he spoke these words, Roosevelt was a national figure, a candidate for the vice presidency, a war hero, the governor of the most powerful state in the union, and a successful author. When the romance of his life began, back in 1883, he had been a young, well-off reformer from New York of uncertain health, who was regarded by his contemporaries as something of a blue stocking and a dandy, and who had not yet worked out the contours of his adult persona.

It is not too great an exaggeration to say that the person who had been known in childhood as Teedie and in his first marriage as Teddy *became* Theodore Roosevelt in the American West. "There were all kinds of things I was afraid of at first," Roosevelt wrote in his *Autobiography,* "ranging from grizzly bears to 'mean' horses and gun-fighters; but by acting as if I was not afraid I gradually ceased to be afraid." [2] Few individuals have ever tested themselves as often, as cheerfully, and as punishingly as did Theodore Roosevelt. In his own self-mythology, Roosevelt transformed himself in the West from a fragile urbanite into a man who shot grizzly bears at point blank range and punched out drunken gunslingers in saloons.

When Roosevelt first ventured into the Dakota badlands he was a "slim, anemic looking young fellow dressed in an exaggerated style," [3] a local storekeeper said. When his badlands years ended, his ranch hand Bill Sewall said he was now "as husky as almost any man I have ever seen who wasn't dependent on his arms for his livelihood." [4] A newspaperman wrote, "There was very little of the whilom dude in his rough and easy costume… The slow, exasperating drawl and the unique accent… had disappeared, and in their place is a nervous, energetic manner of talking with the flat accent of the West." [5]

Theodore Roosevelt was an easterner who came to regard himself as, "at heart," a westerner too. He was born in New York City on October 27, 1858. He grew up in New York and Long Island. His family took extended tours of Europe and the Middle East. He lived for part of a year in Dresden, Germany. He attended Harvard University, where he was a member of the exclusive Porcellian Club. He was elected at the age of 23 to the first of three terms he would serve in the New York State Assembly. If ever there was a representative of the eastern establishment, it was Theodore Roosevelt. He told his son Ted in 1903, "I rose like a rocket." But the minute he ventured beyond the 100th meridian in early September 1883, Roosevelt reassigned part of his soul forever to the arid and magnificent region between the Mississippi River and the Rocky Mountains. He was 24 years old. Decades later his young Dakota friend

Lincoln Lang wrote, "Clearly I recall his wild enthusiasm over the Bad Lands… It had taken root in the congenial soil of his consciousness, like an ineradicable, creeping plant, as it were, to thrive and permeate it thereafter." [6] The American West was, for Roosevelt, a stage for fantasy adventures and a land of physical and spiritual regeneration. He lived only a small portion of his life in the Dakota badlands, but he returned to the larger West again and again for the rest of his life, and he took some deep, fundamental satisfaction in regarding himself as a man of the West.

Of the Rushmore four, Roosevelt is the one with the most authentic claim to being a true westerner.

Roosevelt journeyed to Dakota Territory in September 1883 for three reasons. First, he wanted to get a buffalo before they blinked into extinction. The southern herd was virtually gone. His best bet was to find one of the small remnant gangs on the northern Great Plains. Second, in 1883 he could only penetrate into the heart of the Great Plains in one of two ways—along the Union Pacific Railway in central Nebraska or along the just-completed Northern Pacific in Dakota Territory. Had he wanted to hunt for a buffalo in the Black Hills, for example, he would have had to leave the train in Bismarck, Dakota Territory, or at North Platte, Nebraska, and then take a long, dirty, bone-shaking stage coach ride the rest of the

Little Missouri, Da,
Sept 8th 1883

Darling Ubfie,
        Yesterday evening I took the six oclock train from Bismarck, and sat up till ten playing whist with a party of jolly young englishmen. Then I tumbled into my bunk and at two o'clock tumbled out, at Little Missouri station. It was bitterly cold, and it was some time before, grofing about among the four or five shanties which formed the "town", I found the low, small building called the "hotel". There were no lights, but vigorous pounding on the door at last awakened the cursing landlord; he showed me up the un-railed stairs to the second story,

The first page of Roosevelt's first-ever letter from the Dakota badlands, to his wife Alice, September 8, 1883.

way to his destination. As his friend Owen Wister wrote in 1923, "south of the Northern Pacific to the Union Pacific spread a broad gap of empty land unveined by railways, where roads and telegraphs were few and far between, where telephones had not yet come, or the wire fence; scarce any fences were to be seen for a thousand miles, save here and there a wooden one around some man's little house or some man's little grave." [7] Fortunately, the NP could deposit Roosevelt precisely where he was most likely to get one of the few remaining buffalo. Third, he had made the acquaintance of a man named H. H. Gorringe in New York in May 1883. Gorringe, a former naval captain who, among other things, was responsible for bringing Cleopatra's Needle to New York City, had purchased an abandoned U.S. Army cantonment just north of the NP line on the west bank of the Little Missouri River. He offered to accompany Roosevelt on the buffalo hunt. Sometime in August 1883 Gorringe backed out of the trip. By then Roosevelt was so eager to seek the adventure that he made the trip alone.

Roosevelt arrived in the Dakota badlands in the middle of the night on September 7-8, 1883. The just-completed Northern Pacific Railroad delivered him to the bedraggled village of Little Missouri about 3 a.m. He dragged his duffle bag over to the grandly named but exceptionally understated Pyramid Park Hotel, managed to rouse the grumpy proprietor, and bought himself space on one of "eight or ten" cots in an upstairs room known as the bullpen. The next morning he joined the stampede downstairs, washed his hands in a fetid sink, dried them on a filthy towel, and sat down to his first cowboy breakfast. Then he took a stroll around the village of Little Missouri to take a look at the country he had entered after dark. The only image he would have had in his mind before the dawn of September 8 came from Eugene V. Smalley's *History of the Northern Pacific Railroad*, which featured a photograph of what it called Pyramid Park, in hopes of attracting tourists and settlers. Later that day, he wrote a letter to his wife Alice back east. That document records Theodore Roosevelt's first impression of the badlands of Dakota Territory, his first impression, indeed, of the American West.

It is a very desolate place, high, barren hills, scantily clad with coarse grass, and here and there in sheltered places a few stunted cottonwood trees; 'wash-outs' deepening at times into great canyons, and steep cliffs of most curious formation abound everywhere, and it was a marvel to me to see how easily our mustangs scrambled over the frightful ground which we crossed, while trying to get up to the grassy plateaus over which we could gallop. There is very little water, and what there is, is so bitter as to be almost a poison, and really undrinkable. It is so alkaline that the very cows milk tastes of it. [8]

The hunting guide he hired that same day to take him to a buffalo, Joe Ferris, was not sure Roosevelt had the right stuff. "He was a slender young fellow and I had my doubts whether he could stand the long trip," Ferris recalled, "To be honest about it, I expected to have to take care of him on the trip—saddle his horse, show him the customs of the plains, see that he got his grub regularly and the other little things that come up on a hunting trip of the kind." [9] Ferris underestimated Roosevelt. Within two weeks he had changed his mind. Although Ferris admitted that "bad luck followed us like a yellow dog follows a drunkard," he came to admire Roosevelt's stamina, his un-dude-like willingness to perform hard, dirty, exhausting work without complaint, and his perennial good cheer. On that adventure alone Roosevelt crawled hands and face-first into a cactus patch, woke up at dawn one morning in a pool of rainwater, and, when his horse Nell reared suddenly, received a blow to the forehead from the barrel of his rifle that caused him to bleed "like a stuck pig." Still, "after a week he was fresh as a daisy," Ferris admitted, "and I was dead beat." [10] Roosevelt responded to even the worst of his sufferings with characteristic enthusiasm. "By Godfrey, but this is fun!" [11]

Roosevelt traveled to Dakota Territory specifically to kill a buffalo, but almost immediately he fell in love with the badlands of the Little Missouri River Valley. He had not been in the area more than a week before he decided to invest a significant portion of his inheritance in a badlands cattle ranch in today's North Dakota. On September 19, he impulsively wrote a check for $14,000 to purchase cattle for the first of the two badlands cattle ranches he acquired during his Dakota years. Although Roosevelt never actually owned a single acre of North Dakota land, in that twilight era of squatter's rights he purchased first the Maltese Cross Ranch seven miles south of the

NP railway and, less than a year later, a second ranch 35 miles north of the NP that he named the Elkhorn.

Roosevelt spent significant portions of 1883, 1884, 1885, 1886, and 1887 in the Dakota badlands. The longest of his stays was between March 19 and July 8, 1886. Roosevelt extracted much more than immediate satisfaction from his badlands adventures. He wrote many articles and a trilogy of excellent books about his experiences in what he persisted in calling the "Wild West." The chapter on his Dakota years in his 1913 *Autobiography* is one of the best things Roosevelt ever wrote. When he came to recruit a "harum scarum" voluntary cavalry regiment to lead into harm's way in Cuba, Roosevelt recruited cowboys, Indians, and hunters from the American West, many of them acquaintances from his Dakota years. He played the Dakota rancher and cowboy card with startling frequency for the rest of his life. His correspondence and table talk are almost astonishingly studded with badlands references.

From 1884 to 1887 Roosevelt threw himself into the life of the vanishing frontier so completely and with such unabashed self-advertisement that it permanently transformed the way the world thought of him. When William McKinley died of gunshot wounds on September 14, 1901, Roosevelt entered the presidency by the back door. Senator Mark Hanna of Ohio, the kingmaker who had been the principal patron of McKinley's political career, bitterly quipped, "Now look—that damned cowboy is president of the United States." [12] Roosevelt would have liked that. Roosevelt was one of the first presidents to be widely cartooned. It was irresistible to picture him either as a Rough Rider or a cowboy—these Rooseveltian characters were not entirely distinct. Roosevelt was an urban man who self-fashioned himself as a man of the frontier. More than almost any political figure in American history, including Jefferson and Washington, Roosevelt constructed the persona by which he wished to be understood. It is not clear how deliberately political this refashioning was, but the result was that Roosevelt made his intense intellectualism palatable to the American people by removing it from the forefront of his public image, and placing a man of adventure, sometimes reckless adventure, there instead. He gave credibility to his political righteousness by making sure the public never forgot that he was

the kind of man who climbed the Matterhorn on his honeymoon, tracked down desperadoes and brought them to justice, and volunteered for combat service in the Spanish-American War when he could easily have remained behind his desk at the U.S. Navy Department. He wanted to be "that damned cowboy," a larger-than-life, pugnacious, Manichaean, deputy sheriff whose face was marred by dust and sweat and blood.

A mere political opportunist would have established a brief presence in the American West, dabbled in a few tepid adventures, and made the most of them for the rest of his life. Today it is not uncommon for a wealthy, ambitious, or prominent man to own a little ranch somewhere out West and to be seen, from time to time, clearing brush on his estate. That was not Theodore Roosevelt. Roosevelt engaged in activities that few other men could or would endure. It's hard to imagine any other president of the United States who could keep up with him in reckless strenuosity, including Andrew Jackson, George Washington, or Dwight Eisenhower. Roosevelt ranched in the West, tramped in the West (with John Burroughs, among others), hunted for big game in the West, photographed the West with his portable camera, wrote extensively about the West, learned some of his conservation ethics in the West, and built one foundation of his national political base in the West.

An individual's character is set long before he is 25 years old. But it is undeniable that the American West deepened Roosevelt's character in measurable ways. The great Roosevelt biographer Edmund Morris has written, "Some extraordinary physical and spiritual transformation occurred during this arduous period. It was as if his adolescent battle for health, and his more recent but equally intense battle against despair, were crowned with sudden victory." [13]

ᚤ ᚤ ᚤ

Roosevelt loved the West in six interrelated ways.

He loved the *emptiness* of the West. In his *Autobiography* he wrote, "It was a land of vast silent spaces, of lonely rivers, and of plains where the wild game stared at the passing horseman." On another occasion, he wrote, "Nowhere, not even at

sea, does a man feel more lonely than when riding over the far reaching, seemingly never-ending plains. Their very vastness and… their melancholy monotony have a strong fascination for me." [14] In 1883 Roosevelt found the emptiness of the West eerily fascinating; by the summer of 1884, after the death of his first wife, he regarded it as a perfect landscape on which to grieve. He said the badlands reminded him somehow of the poetry of Edgar Allan Poe.

He loved the *freedom* of the West. To his sister Bamie he wrote, "I felt as absolutely free as a man could feel. As you know, I do not mind loneliness."[15] To Henry Cabot Lodge he wrote, "I heartily enjoy this life, with its perfect freedom, for I am very fond of hunting and there are few sensations I prefer to that of galloping over these rolling, limitless prairies, rifle in hand, or winding my way among the barren, fantastic or grimly picturesque deserts of the so-called Bad Lands." [16] "I suppose it is right," he wrote more philosophically in *Hunting Trips of a Ranchman,* "and for the best that the great cattle country, with its broad extent of fenceless land, over which the ranchman rides as free as the game that he follows or the horned herds that he guards, should be in the end broken up into small patches of fenced farm land and grazing land; but I hope against hope that I myself shall not live to see this take place, for when it does one of the pleasantest and freest phases of western American life will have come to an end." [17]

He loved the *bigness and magnificence* of the West. In Dickinson, Dakota Territory, on July 4, 1886, he famously said, "Like all Americans, I like big things; big prairies, big forests and mountains, big wheat fields, railroads—and herds of cattle too; big factories, steamboats and everything else." [18] Roosevelt demanded that the people of Dickinson and the nation develop an American character equal to the grandeur of the mountains, rivers, canyons, forests, and fields of the continent, particularly the lands west of the Mississippi River. After visiting the Grand Canyon for the first time in May 1903 he wrote, "I don't exactly know what words to use in describing it. It is beautiful and terrible and unearthly. It made me feel as if I were gazing at a sunset of strange and awful splendor." [19] In Santa Cruz in May 1903 he called the Redwoods and Sequoias "American's cathedrals." He demanded that we treat the sublime features of the American landscape as respectfully as the Europeans maintain Notre Dame, St. Peter's, the Pantheon, or Cologne Cathedral. "A grove of giant redwoods or sequoias should be kept just as we keep a great or beautiful cathedral," he explained. Of his time with John Muir sleeping out under El Capitan in Yosemite National Park, he wrote, "It was like lying in a great solemn cathedral, far vaster and more beautiful than any built by the hand of man."

He loved the *character of the people* he met west of the Mississippi and also the *characters* he encountered. Roosevelt was well aware that the men and women he mingled with in the American West were not his equals in social standing, education, manners, or breadth of outlook. He soon realized, however, that what they lacked in formal culture they more than made up in resourcefulness, discipline, and core strength. Although he always maintained his status as a gentleman, and bristled at gestures of over-familiarity, he found much to admire in the people of the plains. Because his respect and admiration were so undisguised, the people he met soon learned to tolerate—and in many instances admire—Roosevelt. The fact that the people of the frontier were inelegant, plainspoken to the point of bluntness, poetic butchers of standard grammar and usage, and prone to violence somehow appealed to Roosevelt. He loved to tell stories of the endearing lawlessness and waywardness of his acquaintances of that period. Of Hell Roaring Bill Jones, once the sheriff of Billings County, he wrote, "He was a very good official when sober, and a trustworthy, hard-working man while in my employ; but on his occasional sprees he got very drunk indeed and then he swore a great deal and shot occasionally... Happening to learn that he had been a constable in Bismarck but had resigned, I asked him why, whereupon he answered, 'Well, I beat the mayor over the head with my gun one day. The mayor he didn't mind it, but the superintendent of police he said he guessed I'd better resign.'" [20] He loved to tell the story of a man who was in prison for killing a woman. It was an accident, the man told TR. 'I was actually trying to shoot my wife.' Such stories delighted TR. Of frontiersmen, Roosevelt wrote, "Their grim, harsh, narrow lives were yet strangely fascinating, and full of adventurous toil and danger; none but natures as strong, as freedom-loving, and as full of bold defiance as theirs could have endured existence on the terms which these men found pleasurable. Their iron surroundings made a mould which turned out all alike in the same shape." [21]

He loved the *access to big game* that the West afforded him. He killed at least one of everything. By the time he had spent just a few months in the Dakota badlands Roosevelt had killed a buffalo, white tailed deer and mule deer, elk, pronghorn antelope, and bighorn sheep. On December 14, 1884, he wrote to his sister Bamie, "I have now killed every kind of plains game." [22] That summer he had also killed his first grizzly bear in the Big Horn Mountains north of Sheridan, Wyoming. By the time his sojourn in the Dakota badlands ended, however, Roosevelt had come to realize that the big game of the American West would be hunted to extinction if steps weren't taken to sustain their numbers and protect them from what he called game butchery. With his new friend George Bird Grinnell, Roosevelt created the Boone and Crockett Club in 1887 to promote responsible hunting and lobby Congress to pass appropriate conservation legislation, beginning with new protections for Yellowstone National Park.

He loved the physical and spiritual *regenerative powers* of the West. Even as late as the summer before his buffalo hunt, he had had a severe attack of asthma and cholera morbus. The West and the strenuous life seemed to cure him. He assured his mother, his sisters, his friend Henry Cabot Lodge, and anyone else who would listen that since he ventured into the badlands he had "never been in better health." At the end of his buffalo hunt, he wrote his wife Alice, "I have three splendid trophies, and the heads of the buffalo and stags will look grandly in our hall; and I am feeling in such health as I have certainly not been in for the past four years." [23] In his book, *Hunting Trips of a Ranchman,* he wrote of a night he spent out on the range camping alone: "a fire was started for cheerfulness, and some of the coals were raked off apart to cook over... It is wonderful how cosey a camp, in clear weather, becomes if there is a good fire and enough to eat, and how sound the sleep is afterward in the cool air." [24] To Bamie he wrote, "How I do sleep at night now." [25]

Between Roosevelt's first and second visits to the Dakota badlands, his first wife Alice Hathaway Lee died, two days after giving birth to their daughter Alice. His mother Mittie died in the same house on the same day, Valentine's Day 1884. His wife was just 22 years old, his mother 49. In his diary Roosevelt wrote, "The light has gone out of my life." When he returned to the badlands in

June 1884, Roosevelt was playing a different role: the lonely figure of grief. He took endless rides alone through the badlands and plains country. He told his ranch hands that his grief was "beyond healing," that his daughter would be better off under the care of her aunt Bamie, and that he had "nothing to live for." [26] But Roosevelt was so naturally vital and resilient, the frontier was so full of raw life and primitive action, and the land was so open, fresh, and compelling, that he soon recovered his spirits. Probably he intended to grieve longer than he in fact did, but the life force was too strong in him and in the landscape he had chosen as his second home. He wrote, "I grow very fond of this place... at evening I love to sit out in front of the hut and see hard, gray outlines gradually grow soft and purple as the flaming sunset by degrees softens and dies away; while my days I spend generally alone, riding through the lonely rolling prairie and broken lands." His sister Corinne believed that the badlands saved his life. "He threw himself... into the wide untrammeled life of the West," she wrote, "and perhaps those years which he spent in North Dakota were the turning point in his whole existence." [27]

Eventually, Roosevelt could write, with remarkable self-awareness, "Black care seldom sits behind a rider whose pace is fast enough." [28]

ⵖ ⵖ ⵖ

Theodore Roosevelt ventured into the American West in 1883 to kill a buffalo. He was also seeking experience on the borderlands of savagery and civilization, as men of his time liked to think of it. Roosevelt believed that the rapid urbanization of American life in the decades following the Civil War had made American men effeminate and decadent. Like Frederick Jackson Turner, who later became his friend, Roosevelt believed that the Euro-American errand in the wilderness (1607-1890) had created the distinctive American character. The Turner thesis, as it came to be known after 1893, was a little more pastoral than TR's more violent formulation of how the frontier shaped American civilization, but both writers emphasized the capacity of the frontier to renew the American character and break down habits of the heart that had bedeviled European civilization. Roosevelt knew that the frontier phase of American history was coming to an end.

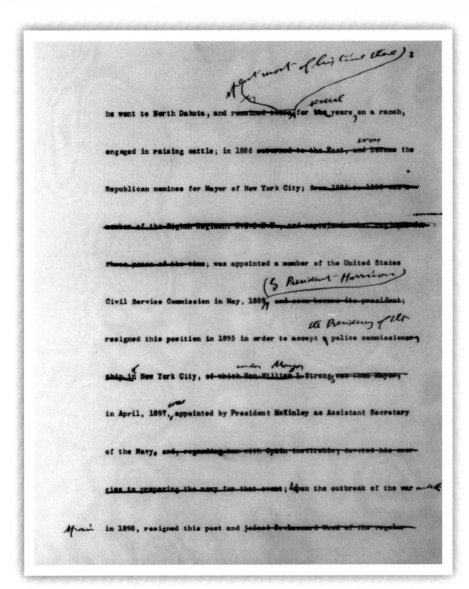

When President Roosevelt read this biographical sketch of his life, he penciled in corrections, emphasizing the time he spent in the Dakota badlands.

Roosevelt believed that an unmediated encounter between frontiersmen and wild nature had been the core of the American experience, that the vanishing of the frontier experience from American life (ca. 1890) could not be good for the American character and—be that as it may—he was going to get as big a gulp of that experience as he could before it was too late. Part of Roosevelt's later love of the National Park idea was that it would perpetuate little islands of American wilderness life, that national parks would make it possible for otherwise tame Americans to enjoy the campfire and the rustling of the cottonwoods after the great bulk of the western landscape had been parceled out and tamed. Camping in Yellowstone would never be quite the same as camping in some undesignated corner of the unfenced, unbounded West, but it was better than dining at Delmonico's

and sleeping on a down mattress in a brownstone or a tenement house.

Roosevelt understood specifically that the cowboy phase of American history could not last long. He began the first of his badlands trilogy, *Hunting Trips of a Ranchman,* with a sociological analysis of the cattle industry. "For we ourselves and the life that we lead will shortly pass away from the plains as completely as the red and white hunters who have vanished from before our herds. The free, open-air life of the ranchman, the pleasantest and healthiest life in America, is from its very nature ephemeral. The broad and boundless prairies have already been bounded and will soon be made narrow. It is scarcely a figure of speech to say that the tide of white settlement during the last few years has risen over the West like a flood; and the cattlemen are but the spray from the crest of the wave, thrown far in advance, but soon to be overtaken." [29] This sounds melancholy, but Roosevelt actually regarded the dynamics he observed in the West as not only inevitable but good. The fact that he was imbibing something that would soon be "'gone, gone with lost Atlantis,' gone to the isle of ghosts and of strange dead memories," [30] gave his experiences a deeper significance and insured his uniqueness in American establishment culture.

It was not just the idea of the West that engaged Roosevelt's heart and soul, however, not merely the possibility that he could be renewed and made more manly by authentic experiences on the frontier. He also clearly fell deeply in love with the grandeur of the West, the vastness of its landscapes, and the magnificence of landforms that had no counterparts east of the Mississippi River. Although he was prone to theorizing about the frontier experience, likening his buckskin adventures to the primordial western experiences of George Rogers Clark, Davy Crockett, and Daniel Boone, Roosevelt's deepest satisfactions

seem to have derived not from books but from raw experience—bathing in a bone-chilling stream, lying out under the stars, squatting before a camp fire eating beans and bacon, listening to the message on the wind or the creaking of saddle leather during a dawn ride. Roosevelt responded to the elemental quality of the American West. He liked to ride out alone for days on end, with hardtack and a few bags of tea, to see what it felt like to be all alone in a wild open country with nobody to help him, dependent on his rifle for food.

In June 1884 he undertook a long solo journey to see if he "could not do perfectly well without a guide." [31] His gear included horse and rifle, a blanket, an oilskin coat in case it rained, a large metal cup, tea and salt and biscuits, and a waterproof bag with a book—he almost never traveled without a book—and other small personal items. "It was wonderful," he wrote, "how cosy a camp, in clear weather, becomes if there is a good fire and enough to eat, and how sound the sleep is afterwards in the cool air, with the brilliant stars glimmering through the branches overhead." [32]

Roughing it is not for everyone. Most of Roosevelt's contemporaries felt that thousands of years of human progress and more recently the Industrial Revolution had liberated humankind from the discomforts of shaving in a cold stream and drinking cowboy coffee around a smoky fire. Many of his contemporaries found the wilderness streak in Roosevelt inexplicable and absurd. Even those who understood how deep the love of outdoor life ran in Roosevelt's character were happy to admire his wood lust from afar. His closest friend Henry Cabot Lodge, for example, was archly amused by Roosevelt's breathless letters about his frontier adventures and his love of the primordial, but the Boston Brahmin never joined Roosevelt on any of his western journeys. Lodge sent his son Bay with the Roosevelts to the badlands and Yellowstone National Park in 1890, but he did not make the journey himself.

Roosevelt never lost his passion for wild country. Although the greater he became the fewer risks he was permitted to take, he never entirely stopped roughing it, though after his presidency he transferred some of his search for primitive adventures to two other continents: Africa (1909-10), and South America (1913-14). In South America things became so intensely raw that Roosevelt nearly lost his life. He had no regrets. The Amazon basin adventure was, he said, "my last chance to be a boy." When he first ventured by train from the east coast of Africa into the interior, Roosevelt was so excited that he sat outside the train engine on a special chair attached to the cowcatcher.

Roosevelt's identification with the West seemed more exotic in his time than it does to us, even though the people of that era were closer to their frontier history than we are. The number of presidents of the United States in the post-Civil War period who enjoyed sleeping out on the hard ground and bathing in an icy stream can be counted on one hand with several fingers to spare.

⅄ ⅄ ⅄

Almost everyone found Roosevelt inauthentic at first—a dubious eastern swell sporting spectacles and an absurd falsetto voice, wearing designer cowboy duds, biting off his words and vociferating "bully," and "by Jove," and "dee-lighted," among the illiterate or half-literate denizens of the badlands country. He was game for anything, but his manners seemed somehow comic and improbable to the hardened residents of the frontier. Still, he was so dogged in his determination to be accepted, so willing to get back up on the horse, perform the most difficult and exhausting chores, that virtually everyone wound up liking and admiring him. After a few days' acquaintance in 1883, when Roosevelt started back towards the NP railroad with his buffalo trophy, the Scottish ranch manager Gregor Lang said, "There goes the most remarkable man I ever met." [33] His son Lincoln Lang, just 16 years old when he met Roosevelt, later wrote a superb book-length tribute to his friendship with Roosevelt. In *Ranching with Roosevelt,* Lang wrote, "It was listening to those talks after supper in the old shack on the Cannonball that I first came to understand that the Lord made the earth for all of us, and not for a chosen few." [34] The editor of the *Bad Lands Cow Boy,* after observing TR address the citizens of Dickinson on the Fourth of July 1886 and listening to him talk political reform on the train all the way from Medora to Dickinson, and then from Dickinson back to Medora, predicted that Roosevelt would one day become the president of the United States. A skeptical Montana hunting guide quickly overcame his condescension towards Roosevelt and decided that he was "the gamest

man I have ever known," even though TR lectured the professional hunter sternly about the evils of killing game merely for pecuniary gain. "There was something of the savor of the West in his manner and his frankness, and, so long as I could keep my eyes away from his foolish pants, I cottoned to the things he said and the way he said them. In about an hour he had made me forget his knickers and had won me over as far as I would ever go for any man." [35]

Roosevelt was always something of a caricature of himself. He loved to tell stories of his adventures, including comic adventures or adventures that put him in less than heroic light. But he also unquestionably had the *right stuff.* He made the most of his western experiences and probably he exaggerated some of his experiences to the limit of their credibility, but the events he describes certainly occurred.

He really did punch out a drunken gunslinger in a saloon in Wibaux, Montana, then known as Mingusville. He really did track down the three boat thieves, one of them a potentially dangerous man, arrest them in the middle of nowhere, and march them to justice in Dickinson, Dakota Territory. He really did get bucked off of unbroken horses, one of which threw him so hard that he broke the point of his shoulder. He really did spend more than a month on a badlands cattle roundup, where he really did help stop a stampede.

When he delivered the boat thieves to the sheriff in Dickinson, on April 11, 1886, he was so exhausted and his feet were so blistered from the ordeal that he sought immediate medical attention. After a chance meeting with the town physician Dr. Victor Hugo Stickney ("By George, then you're exactly the man I want to see"), Roosevelt got his feet lanced and bandaged. Fortunately, Dr. Stickney wrote an account of his first meeting with the future president. "He… had had no sleep for forty-eight hours, and he was all teeth and eyes; but even so he seemed a man unusually wide-awake. You could see he was thrilled by the adventures he had been through… He was just like a boy." [36]

Roosevelt sought authenticity so purposefully that he took risks that most people of his class would never undertake.

The story of Roosevelt punching out the gunslinger in the bar in Wibaux has a kind of dime

novel quality to it. But lest one think Roosevelt was making these stories up, or weaving a mock-epic upon very slender foundations, it should be remembered that in August 1889 in the Big Hole Basin in southwestern Montana, TR and his guide John Willis found themselves in a roadhouse where a group of tough lumberjacks were carousing. When TR asked a woodsman to pass the porridge, the fellow made the mistake of calling Roosevelt a "four-eyed gink." Roosevelt erupted from his chair and, according to John Willis, knocked out two hardened loggers with his fisticuffs. [37] Nobody likes to be called a gink.

Roosevelt was the sort of man who needed to test himself—against other men, against nature and its creatures, and against his own physical and mental limitations. One day Roosevelt tried to ride his horse along the narrow lip of a submerged dam in the Little Missouri River when it was still brimmed with running ice. Roosevelt's horse slipped and fell into the frigid stream. Roosevelt jumped off Manitou (his favorite horse) and swam the horse to shore, guiding it through the ice floes. A few days later he swam across the frigid river again with Manitou, just to make sure he could do it.

On a hunting trip in Idaho, TR fell off a mountain ledge and plunged 60 feet through pine tree branches to a shelf below. His guide John Willis said, "I turned around just in time to see him disappear… head foremost over the sharp edge, with his rifle still in his hand. I wouldn't have given two bits for his life." [38] The pine trees apparently cushioned his fall, for Roosevelt suffered no more than cuts and bruises, though he was momentarily stunned. On the same trip, TR had his two companions lower him by rope down a cliff so that he could photograph a particularly beautiful waterfall from just the right angle. They discovered that they were unable to haul him back up to safety. Eventually Willis scrambled down to the stream below, fashioned a makeshift raft, and then TR's other companion cut the rope and let him plunge 40 feet into the stream. Although Roosevelt sustained bruised ribs and other injuries, he insisted on finishing the hunt once Willis fished him out of the stream.

On more than one occasion, Roosevelt had loaded guns pointed at him. Hunting on the Montana-Idaho-Wyoming border in the early fall of 1889, TR returned to camp to find his guide Hank Griffin sitting drunk with his back to a tree.

Griffin cocked his rifle, pointed it at TR, and ordered the tenderfoot to walk back to Helena alone, a distance of several hundred miles. TR quietly walked to his pack pony, pulled out a rifle, sneaked up on the drunken guide, and disarmed him at point blank range. He then gathered up his gear and set off alone—on horseback—towards Helena. [39]

Roosevelt was involved in at least two stampedes, one during the Little Missouri roundup in 1884, and one, in the spring of 1885, when he was working 1,500 new head of cattle north from the NP railroad tracks to the Elkhorn Ranch:

The only salvation was to keep them close together, as, if they once got scattered, we knew they could never be gathered; so I kept on one side, and the cowboy on the other, and never in my life did I ride so hard. In the darkness I could but dimly see the shadowy outlines of the herd, as with whip and spurs I ran the pony along its edge, turning back the beasts at one point barely in time to heel and keep them in at another. The ground was cut up by numerous little gullies, and each of us got several falls, horses and riders turning complete somersaults. We were dripping with sweat, and our ponies quivering and trembling like quaking aspens, when, after more than an hour of the most violent exertion, we finally got the herd quieted again. [40]

It doesn't get any more authentic than this. This is not the sort of experience one can buy at a dude ranch. These were the adventures of a man who was told by his physician in 1880 that his health was so fragile that he should never even bound up a flight of stairs.

ㄚ ㄚ ㄚ

Roosevelt's sojourn in the Dakota badlands effectively ended in 1887. His marriage to Edith Carow (December 2, 1886), coupled with the killing winter of 1886-87, had the effect of lessening his attachment to ranches so far from the centers of American power, finance, and literature. Edith was a woman of great physical energy, but she was not the sort of woman who would want to cast her lot on the western frontier. Among other things, Edith was less able to

overcome class bias than her husband, who became something of a limited social democrat in the equalitarian atmosphere of the American West. Roosevelt continued to maintain cattle herds after 1887, but he never again gave his ranches the full measure of his attention or enthusiasm. By 1898 when he was preparing for his adventure in Cuba, he effectively gave up cattle ranching altogether.

Roosevelt lost a good deal of money in Dakota Territory, but he never regretted his decision to find a second home along the banks of the Little Missouri River. His ranch manager Bill Sewall said, "I don't believe he ever made a dollar out of his cattle... It had brought him to his physical prime. He weighed about one hundred and fifty pounds, and it was clear bone, muscle and grit. The ranch undoubtedly made his career possible." Sewall said TR's sojourn in the West "undoubtedly saved Theodore Roosevelt's life and reason." [41]

Roosevelt always exaggerated the amount of time he spent in Dakota Territory. Although the total number of days he spent there amounted to less than one full calendar year, he claimed that he had, at minimum, spent the better part of five years there, and as time went on the experience grew in his imagination until he reckoned he had spent seven years, even most of ten years (once, 15 years!), ranching and hunting in today's North Dakota. It seems likely that Roosevelt was not attempting to deceive his friends or the American public when he made these claims. His experiences in North Dakota were so important to his sense of himself, so critical to the transformation that made him the Theodore Roosevelt of American mythology, and so compelling to the American public, that Roosevelt probably came to see them as longer in duration than in fact they were. In 1904 President Roosevelt asked New Mexico Senator Albert Fall, "Do you know what chapter in all my life looking back over all of it I would choose to remember, where the alternative forced upon me to recall [only] one portion of it, and to have erased from my memory all other experiences? I would take the memory of my life on the ranch with its experiences close to nature and among the men who lived nearest her." [42]

ㄚ ㄚ ㄚ

It is always difficult to sort out caricature and authenticity in Theodore Roosevelt. Although his verifiable adventures insure his frontier

credentials, there remains something uncannily *literary* about his western experience. He borrowed the phrase "the romance of my life," from the adventure novelist Thomas Mayne Reid's *The Scalp Hunters.* [43] He borrowed the phrase "my crowded hour," from a poem by Walter Scott. [44] His written accounts of his adventures read like episodes in a dime novel. It is not quite that he was distorting his actual experiences for narrative effect—though no doubt sometimes he was—but rather that he actually tried to live his life like the hero of those stories, like a character from John Bunyan's *Pilgrim's Progress.* Perhaps because during the years of his childhood invalidism he could only experience the life of a strong and healthy boy vicariously through fiction, including boys' fiction, Roosevelt locked a part of himself permanently into that boys' fantasy persona, and rode it with remarkable success through life.

From his ranch in Dakota Territory he wrote to his sister Corinne, "I am greatly attached to the ranch and the life out here, and am really fond of the men... we are so rarely able to actually in real life, dwell in our ideal 'hero land.' The loneliness and freedom... out here appeals to me very powerfully." [45]

In 1903 President Roosevelt took a 14,000-mile train trip through the American West. He visited 25 states and gave 262 speeches. The journey took him briefly to Medora, for two weeks to Yellowstone National Park (with John Burroughs), for three days to Yosemite National Park (with John Muir), to the Grand Canyon, to the California redwoods, to Sharon Springs, Kansas, to the rough mining town of Butte, Montana, and everywhere in between. He was gone from Washington, D.C., from April 1 until June 5. Later that summer, when he was back in his routine in the White House, Roosevelt wrote a splendid 28-page letter to Secretary of State John Hay recounting his travels. That letter of August 9, 1903, is one of Roosevelt's finest. Among other things, it provides essential details nowhere else reported about Roosevelt's time in the Dakota badlands between 1883-87. But what makes it so remarkable is that Roosevelt cast the letter somewhat in the manner of John Hay's *Pike County Ballads,* the collection of sentimental poems about unsophisticated but admirable heartland folks Hay had published in 1871. In other words, in his endless letter describing his recent journey and recounting the adventures of his formative years in the West, Roosevelt was trying to impress Hay, whom he admired more as a man of letters than as a diplomat, by turning his adventures in the West into a literary achievement.

> At Medora, which we reached after dark, the entire population of the Bad Lands down to the smallest baby had gathered to meet me. This was formerly my home station. The older men and women I knew well; the younger ones had been wild towheaded children when I lived and worked along the Little Missouri. I had spent nights in their ranches. I still remembered meals which the women had given me when I had come from some hard expedition, half famished and sharpset as a wolf. I had killed buffalo and elk, deer and antelope with some of the men. With others I had worked on the trail, on the calf roundup, on the beef roundup. We had been together on occasions which we still remembered when some bold rider met his death in trying to stop a stampede, in riding a mean horse, or in the quicksands of some swollen river which he sought to swim. They all felt I was their man, their old friend; and even if they had been hostile to me in the old days when we were divided by the sinister bickering and jealousies and hatreds of all frontier communities, they now firmly believed they had always been my staunch friends and admirers. [46]

This is one of the finest and most poignant passages Roosevelt ever wrote.

David McCullough has shown that Roosevelt saw many of his own western experiences through the lens of his hero Francis Parkman (1823-1893), to whom he dedicated his magnum opus, *The Winning of the West.* Where Parkman reported that the Great Plains make "the very shadow of civilization" seem "a hundred leagues behind," Roosevelt wrote, "Civilization seems as remote as if we were living in an age long past." Where Parkman saw in the endless plains "green undulation like motionless swells of the ocean," Roosevelt reported that "the grassland stretches out in the sunlight like the sea." [47] And so on.

In August 1884, to his closest friend Henry Cabot Lodge, Roosevelt wrote, "It would electrify some of my friends who have accused me of representing the kid-glove element in politics if

they could see me galloping over the plains day in and day out, clad in a buckskin shirt and leather chaparajos, with a big sombrero on my head." [48] This delightful passage makes clear that Roosevelt not only liked being an "authentic cowboy," but picturing himself as one. Even better, he liked imagining others picturing him in buckskin and sombrero. Roosevelt was a complicated man. The narrative he constructed of his life was so colorful and compelling that it is easy to reduce him to a caricature. Indeed, he frequently did so himself. It is a mistake to assume a reductionist understanding of Roosevelt, however. He may have seemed like an overgrown boy ("You must always remember that the President is about six," said his friend Cecil Spring Rice), but there was an extremely serious adult behind the comic persona. Roosevelt was a towering intellectual, possibly the best reader among American presidents, and certainly the most prolific writer. More than most individuals, he saw the world through books. His *Autobiography* has more references to the books he owned and read than the memoirs of any other president, and probably more than all of them combined. Roosevelt was a wonderful, loving, hands-on father, and sometimes an oppressive one. He pushed his eldest son Ted until he suffered a nervous breakdown. He loved all creatures great and small and killed far more than his share. He had a nuanced view of international affairs, but in Cuba he could exult, "Look at those damned Spanish dead." He was the most confident politician of his era and yet as the 1904 election neared there were moments when he was pretty sure he would be defeated. Biographers have detected a serious streak of depression behind the bully surface. No matter how simplistic his rhetoric, Roosevelt seldom failed to appreciate the complexity of the world over which he presided.

Ɏ Ɏ Ɏ

When he got his hands on the reins of power, Roosevelt did everything he could for the American West. In his first annual message to Congress, December 3, 1901, he devoted several long passages to conservation measures, a clear break with his predecessor McKinley, whose policies he had vowed faithfully to maintain in the three years, 171 days following McKinley's assassination. The new president called for better

management of the national forests, a greatly enlarged federal forest system, the need for federally funded dams and irrigation systems in the arid lands of the American West. Roosevelt wrote, "The fundamental idea of forestry is the perpetuation of forests by use. Forest protection is not an end of itself; it is a means to increase and sustain the resources of our country and the industries which depend upon them. The preservation of our forests is an imperative business necessity. We have come to see clearly that whatever destroys the forest, except to make way for agriculture, threatens our well being."

As president, Roosevelt doubled the number of national parks from five to ten; added 150 million acres to the national forest system and placed the management of the forests in the U.S. Department of Agriculture; signed the Antiquities Act on June 8, 1906, and proclaimed the first 18 National Monuments, beginning with Devils Tower and eventually including the Grand Canyon, at 828,000 acres. He invented the National Wildlife Refuge System and designated the first 51, beginning with Pelican Island, Florida, on March 14, 1903. He signed the Newlands Reclamation Act and named the first 24 federal irrigation projects, one of which, the Salt River Project in Arizona, led to the construction of the mammoth Roosevelt Dam, then the largest masonry dam in the world. In 1911, at the dedication of the dam, Roosevelt declared that the reclamation act and the Panama Canal were the principal "material" achievements of his presidency. In 1908, Roosevelt convened the first-ever White House Governors Conference— designed to serve as an inventory and status report on America's natural resources.

Ɏ Ɏ Ɏ

It would be difficult to tally up how many journeys Roosevelt made into the American West in the course of his lifetime, how many speeches he gave in how many cities, villages, and trackside platforms, how many quadrupeds he shot in how many states, how many words he wrote about the West, what percentage of his conversation it came to occupy. It is safe to say that Roosevelt killed something in almost every state west of the Mississippi River, that he rode a horse in most of those states, and that he slept in primitive conditions that no other president would have endured—in North and South Dakota, Arizona, Montana, Idaho, Colorado, Wyoming, Texas, New Mexico, and California.

He is widely regarded as one of America's greatest conservationists, certainly one of the handful of greatest conservationists among presidents of the United States. His Elkhorn Ranch (sans buildings) has been preserved by the National Park Service and by the U.S. Forest Service. It is certainly one of the shrines of the American conservation movement, still one of the most remote and beautiful places in the American West, and the crown jewel of Theodore Roosevelt National Park.

In the American West Roosevelt found his health, his adult persona, his conservation ethic, and one of the principal arenas in which to strive valiantly. First the American West transformed Theodore Roosevelt. Then Roosevelt transformed the American West.

Clay S. Jenkinson

Theodore Roosevelt Scholar-in-Residence
The Theodore Roosevelt Center
Dickinson State University

# FOOTNOTES

[1] Quoted in James F. Vivian, ed., *The Romance of My Life: Theodore Roosevelt's Speeches in Dakota* (Fargo: Theodore Roosevelt Medora Foundation, 1989), 30.

[2] Theodore Roosevelt, *Autobiography* (New York: Library of America, 2004), 306-07.

[3] Quoted in Michael Collins, *That Damned Cowboy: Theodore Roosevelt and the American West* (London: Peter Lang, 1990), 29.

[4] Quoted in Edmund Morris, *The Rise of Theodore Roosevelt* (New York: Modern Library, 1979), 297.

[5] Quoted in Morris, *The Rise of Theodore Roosevelt*, 297.

[6] Quoted in Morris, *The Rise of Theodore Roosevelt*, 211.

[7] Quoted in Stacy Cordery, *Theodore Roosevelt in the Vanguard of the Modern* (Belmont, CA: Wadsworth/Thomson Learning, 2003), 25.

[8] Roosevelt to Alice Roosevelt, September 8, 1883. Theodore Roosevelt Collection, Houghton Library, Harvard University.

[9] Quoted in Roger L. Di Silvestro, *Theodore Roosevelt in the Badlands: A Young Politician's Quest for Recovery in the American West* (New York: Walker & Company), 44.

[10] Quoted in Collins, *That Damned Cowboy*, 19.

[11] Quoted in Carleton Putnam, *Theodore Roosevelt, Volume One: The Formative Years, 1858-1886* (New York: Charles Scribner's Sons, 1958), 457.

[12] See Richard D. White, Jr., *Roosevelt the Reformer: Theodore Roosevelt as Civil Service Commissioner 1889-1895* (Tuscaloosa: University of Alabama Press, 2003), 167.

[13] Morris, *The Rise of Theodore Roosevelt*, 296-97.

[14] Quoted in Collins, *That Damned Cowboy*, 35.

[15] Quoted in Putnam, *Theodore Roosevelt: The Formative Years*, 457.

[16] Quoted in Nathan Miller, *Theodore Roosevelt: A Life* New York: William Murrow, 1992), 162.

[17] Theodore Roosevelt, *Hunting Trips of a Ranchman* (New York: Modern Library, 2004), 37-38.

[18] James A. Vivian, *The Romance of My Life: Theodore Roosevelt's Speeches in Dakota*, 9.

[19] Roosevelt to John Hay, August 9, 1903. See Elting E. Morison, ed., *The Letters of Theodore Roosevelt*, 8 vols. (Cambridge: Harvard University Press, 1951-54), III, 557.

[20] Roosevelt to John Hay, August 9, 1903.

[21] Theodore Roosevelt, *The Winning of the West*, 4 vols. (Lincoln: University of Nebraska Press, 1995), I, 109.

[22] Quoted in Di Silvestro, *Theodore Roosevelt in the Badlands*, 254.

[23] Quoted in Di Silvestro, *Theodore Roosevelt in the Badlands*, 58-59.

[24] Quoted in Putnam, *Theodore Roosevelt: The Formative Years*, 457.

[25] Quoted in Collins, *That Damned Cowboy*, 25.

[26] See Collins, *That Damned Cowboy*, 38.

[27] Quoted in Collins, *That Damned Cowboy*, 157.

[28] Theodore Roosevelt, *Ranch Life and the Hunting Trail* (Lincoln: University of Nebraska Press, 1983), 59.

[29] Roosevelt, *Hunting Trips of a Ranchman*, 26.

[30] Roosevelt, *Autobiography*, 346.

[31] Roosevelt to Anna Roosevelt, quoted in Di Silvestro, *Theodore Roosevelt in the Badlands*, 95.

[32] Quoted in Di Silvestro, *Theodore Roosevelt in the Badlands*, 97-98.

[33] Quoted in Putnam, *Theodore Roosevelt: The Formative Years*, 346.

[34] Quoted in Collins, *That Damned Cowboy*, 17.

[35] Quoted in Di Silvestro, *Theodore Roosevelt in the Badlands*, 222.

[36] Quoted in Di Silvestro, *Theodore Roosevelt in the Badlands*, 208.

[37] Collins, *That Damned Cowboy*, 113.

[38] Quoted in Collins, *That Damned Cowboy*, 84.

[39] See Collins, *That Damned Cowboy*, 114.

[40] Quoted in Morris, *The Rise of Theodore Roosevelt*, 295.

[41] Quoted in Cordery, *Theodore Roosevelt in the Vanguard of the Modern*, 29.

[42] Quoted in Frederick Wood, *Roosevelt as We Knew Him* (Philadelphia: John C. Winston, 1927), 12.

[43] Collins, *That Damned Cowboy*, 8-9.

[44] Sarah Watts, *Rough Rider in the White House* (Chicago: University of Chicago, 2003), 165.

[45] Quoted in Collins, *That Damned Cowboy*, 79.

[46] Morrison, *The Letters of Theodore Roosevelt*, III, 551-52.

[47] David McCullough, *Mornings on Horseback: The Story of an Extraordinary Family, A Vanished Way of Life, and the Unique Child Who Became Theodore Roosevelt* (New York: Simon and Schuster, 1981), 330.

[48] Quoted in Morris, *The Rise of Theodore Roosevelt*, 273.

Roosevelt before the great transformation, ca. 1881.

"I was sent off by myself to Moosehead Lake. On the stage-coach ride thither I encountered a couple of other boys who were about my own age, but very much more competent and also much more mischievous. I have no doubt they were good-hearted boys, but they were boys! They found that I was a foreordained and predestined victim, and industriously proceeded to make life miserable for me. The worst feature was that when I finally tried to fight them I discovered that either one singly could not only handle me with easy contempt, but handle me so as not to hurt me much and yet to prevent my doing any damage whatever in return…

I made up my mind that I must try to learn so that I would not again be put in such a helpless position."

*Autobiography*

# THEODORE ROOSEVELT: 98-POUND WEAKLING

Theodore Roosevelt was not always the exemplar of the strenuous life, not always a man who killed a mountain lion with a knife, who climbed the Matterhorn on his honeymoon, or shot a grizzly bear from point blank range.

As a boy in New York City, Roosevelt was beset with life-threatening asthma and digestive issues that the family called *cholera morbus*.

When he was 12 years old, his father Theodore Roosevelt, Sr., sent him away from the foul air of Manhattan to Moosehead Lake in Maine for the fresh air and outdoor activities available there. On the stagecoach to Maine, two boys, discovering that the frail TR "was a foreordained and predestined victim," bullied him without mercy. "The worst thing," TR wrote 40 years later, "was that when I finally tried to fight them I discovered that either one singly could not only handle me with easy contempt, but handle me so as not to hurt me much and yet prevent my doing any damage whatever in return."

Roosevelt determined that he would never be so helpless again.

That same year, TR's father challenged the future president. "You have the mind but you have not the body, and without the help of the body the mind cannot go as far as it should, You must *make* your body." With his piping voice, Teedie replied, "I will papa. I will make my body."

Roosevelt, Sr., installed a gymnasium upstairs at TR's boyhood home at 28 East 20th Street. TR learned to lift weights. He took boxing lessons. He learned to wrestle. Slowly, he began to transform himself from a feeble child into a reasonably fit young man. What his body lacked in strength, stamina, and athleticism, he made up for in iron willpower, a refusal to be what he called a sniveling invalid, and an almost pathological need to please his father, "the greatest man I ever knew and the only man I ever feared."

> " Man does become fearless by sheer dint of practicing fearlessness. "
>
> — THEODORE ROOSEVELT

By the time he completed his studies at Harvard, in 1880, Roosevelt was a serious hunter, wrestler, boxer, and mountain climber. If he was not exactly the epitome

Roosevelt's will was always his strongest muscle.

of virile young manhood, he was fearless and unwilling to quit, no matter how difficult the conditions. "Man does become fearless," he wrote, "by sheer dint of practicing fearlessness."

Even so, when he had a complete physical exam just before graduating from Harvard, TR was given a stern warning by his physician Dr. Dudley A. Sargeant. He told TR that his heart was weak, that he must beware of too much exertion, that he should, in fact, avoid even running up a flight of stairs.

"Doctor," Roosevelt said, "I am going to do all the things you tell me not to do. If I've got to live the sort of life you have described, I don't care how short it is."

When Roosevelt arrived in the badlands of Dakota in September 1883, he was a bespectacled, thin, fragile-looking man of 24. But he was lion-hearted and ready for adventure.

Listening to Roosevelt at Providence, Rhode Island, 1902.

"I am just an ordinary man without any special ability in any direction. In most things I am just above the average; in some of them a little under, rather than over. I am only an ordinary walker. I can't run. I am not a good swimmer, although I am a strong one. I probably ride better than I do anything else, but I am certainly not a remarkably good rider. I am not a good shot. My eyesight is not strong, and I have to get close to my game in order to make any shot at all. I never could be a good boxer, although I like to box and do keep at it, whenever I can. My eyesight prevents me from ever being a good tennis player, even if otherwise I could qualify. So you see that from the physical point of view I am just an ordinary, or perhaps a little less than ordinary man... I am not a brilliant writer. I have written a great deal, but I always have to work and slave over everything I write. The things that I have done, in one office, or another, are all, with the possible exception of the Panama Canal, just such things as any ordinary man could have done. There is nothing brilliant or outstanding in my record, except, perhaps, this one thing. Whatever I think it is right for me to do, I do."

January 1909
reported by Oscar King Davis

# THE WAY OTHERS SAW ROOSEVELT

Everyone who met Theodore Roosevelt realized there was something remarkable about him, something larger than life. Everyone shared badlands rancher Gregor Lang's first impression in 1883: "There goes the most extraordinary man I ever met."

Almost everyone saw Roosevelt as a man of destiny.

British historian James Bryce said simply, "Theodore Roosevelt is the hope of American politics." William Allen White, editor of the *Emporia Gazette* in Kansas, said, "He is the coming American of the twentieth century."

Some saw Roosevelt as preachy or righteous, or as a towering egotist who could be annoying in his need to dominate. Roosevelt's friend Henry Adams famously said that TR possessed "that singular quality that belongs to ultimate matter—the quality that medieval theology assigned to God—he was Pure Act."

When Henry Cabot Lodge pressed newly elected President Benjamin Harrison to name TR a U.S. civil commissioner, Harrison grumbled that Roosevelt "was impatient to reform everything, between the sunrise and sunset of one day."

Speaker of the House of Representatives Thomas B. Reed wrote wryly to Roosevelt, "If there is one thing more than another for which I admire you, Theodore, it is your original discovery of the Ten Commandments."

Rudyard Kipling spent an evening with Roosevelt at Washington, D.C.'s Cosmos Club. "I curled up on the seat opposite," the great British writer recalled, "and listened and wondered until the universe seemed to be spinning around and Theodore was the spinner."

Many saw Roosevelt as unnecessarily bellicose.

Secretary of State John Hay was one of the most

The bride at every wedding, the corpse at every funeral.

intellectually gifted men of his time. He had been a friend of TR's father Thee. Hay was more than a little skeptical of the younger Roosevelt and was well aware of Roosevelt's imperialist urges and thirst for war. During a crisis involving Chile in 1892, Hay said, "For two nickels he would declare war—shut up the Civil Service Commission, and wage it sole."

Nobody doubted that Roosevelt had faults, but almost everyone found him enormously entertaining and delightful (in small quantities!).

> " My father wanted to be the bride at every wedding, and the corpse at every funeral. "
>
> — ALICE ROOSEVELT

*New York Times* reporter Bayard Hale, wrote, "A hundred times a day the President will laugh, and, when he laughs

he does it with the same energy with which he talks. It is usually a roar of laughter, and it comes nearly every five minutes. His face grows red with merriment, his eyes nearly close, his utterance becomes choked and sputtery and falsetto, and sometimes he doubles up in paroxysm. You don't smile with Mr. Roosevelt; you shout with laughter with him."

Roosevelt's close friend Cecil Spring-Rice, the British ambassador, told a perplexed fellow diplomat, "You must always remember that the president is about six."

The two greatest things ever said of Roosevelt epitomize his character. An admirer from Texas said, "Almost anyone can become the President of the United States, but Theodore Roosevelt could be elected marshall in any town in Texas."

And Roosevelt's colorful and rebellious daughter Alice supposedly said, "My father wanted to be the bride at every wedding, and the corpse at every funeral."

The Roosevelts before Quentin: TR, Archie, Ted, Alice, Kermit, Edith, and Ethel.

"There are many kinds of success in life worth having. It is exceedingly interesting and attractive to be a successful businessman, or railroad man, or farmer, or a successful lawyer or doctor; or a writer, or a President, or a ranchman, or the colonel of a fighting regiment, or to kill grizzly bears and lions. But for unflagging interest and enjoyment, a household of children, if things go reasonably well, certainly makes all other forms of success and achievement lose their importance by comparison."

*Autobiography*

# THEODORE ROOSEVELT AND HIS CHILDREN

Theodore Roosevelt loved children. His own, and those of everyone around him. Perhaps this was in part because there was a good deal of the child in him throughout his life.

Roosevelt's friend Cecil Spring-Rice, the British ambassador, once told a fellow diplomat, "You must always remember that the president is about six."

Roosevelt had six children and two wives. His first wife Alice died on Valentine's Day 1884 just two days after giving birth to her only child, the famous Alice Roosevelt Longworth. Roosevelt's second wife Edith, his childhood sweetheart, bore five children in ten years: Ted (1887), Kermit (1889), Ethel (1891), Archibald (1894), and Quentin (1897).

"There are many kinds of success worth having," Theodore Roosevelt wrote. "It is exceedingly interesting and attractive to be a successful business man, or railroad man, or farmer, or a successful lawyer or doctor; or a writer, or a President, or a ranchman, or the colonel of a fighting regiment, or to kill grizzly bears and lions. But for unflagging interest and enjoyment, a household of children, if things go reasonably well, certainly makes all other forms of success and achievement lose their importance by comparison."

Although he was exceedingly busy, Roosevelt was never a detached father. He loved to roughhouse with his children, join them in pranks, take them camping and hiking, cook meals for them in the wild or on the beach, tell them ghost stories or provide accounts of his adventures in the American West, and to read them books.

Even while serving as president, Roosevelt carved out time to play with his children. "I play bear with the children almost every night," he wrote, "and some

The Roosevelt family in formal portrait.

child is invariably fearfully damaged in the play; but this does not seem to affect the ardor of their enjoyment."

> "I promised the boys I'd go shooting with them at four o'clock, and I never keep the boys waiting."
>
> — THEODORE ROOSEVELT

One afternoon President Roosevelt was in the middle of a meeting when a timid little knock was heard at his office door. The president was informed by his son that it was four o'clock. "We'll finish this talk some other time," Roosevelt told his visitor as he hustled him out. "I promised the boys I'd go shooting with them at four o'clock, and I never keep the boys waiting."

White House play became so animated that it frequently required the chief executive of the United States to change his linens. "The other night before the Diplomatic dinner," he wrote, "having about fifteen minutes to spare, I went into the nursery, where the two small persons in pink tommies instantly raced for the bed and threw themselves on it with ecstatic conviction that a romp was going to begin. I did not have the heart to disappoint them, and the result was that my shirt got so mussed that I had to change it."

For all of this, Roosevelt had very high standards of behavior for his children. TR was not afraid to apply his hand to their backsides when it was deemed necessary. He pushed oldest son Ted so hard that he had "kind of a nervous breakdown." TR was so ashamed for coming on too strong that he resolved, "Hereafter I shall never press Ted either in body or mind." It was a short-lived resolution.

When World War I began, Roosevelt told his sons in no uncertain terms that they were going to go to war and not hold back in desk jobs. His youngest and favorite son, Quentin, did not return from that war.

Roosevelt regarded Jefferson as a visionary unfit for the presidency.

"Washington and Lincoln set the standard of conduct for the public servants of this people. They showed how men of the strongest type could also possess all the disinterested, all the unselfish, devotion to duty and to the interests of their fellow countrymen that we have a right to expect, but can only hope to see in the very highest type of public service. At however great a distance, I have been anxious to follow in their footsteps."

To George Otto Trevelyan
November 6, 1908

"Jefferson, though a man whose views and theories had a profound influence upon our national life, was perhaps the most incapable executive that ever filled the presidential chair; being almost purely a visionary, he was utterly unable to grapple with the slightest actual danger, and, not even excepting his successor, Madison, it would be difficult to imagine a man less fit to guide the State with honor and safety through the stormy times that marked the opening of the present century."

*The Naval War of 1812*

# THEODORE ROOSEVELT AND MOUNT RUSHMORE

**M**ount Rushmore was carved (with dynamite) in the heart of the Black Hills of South Dakota by sculptor Gutzon Borglum. It is the only sculpture of Theodore Roosevelt equal to his outsized personality.

The carving of the four presidents, which began in 1927, was completed in 1941. It was conceived by historian Doane Robinson in 1923 to promote tourism in South Dakota. Robinson persuaded the sculptor Gutzon Borglum to take on the massive project. Robinson's original conception was that sculptures of legendary figures of the American West would be carved on the tops of the Black Hills' celebrated granite needles. Fortunately, the needles proved to be too thin for the project. Borglum himself chose Mount Rushmore, named after a New York lawyer, partly because of its southeastern exposure. The sculptor chose to depict Washington, Jefferson, Lincoln, and Roosevelt for their roles in preserving the American republic and expanding its destiny into the American West.

Washington was dedicated on July 4, 1934, Jefferson in 1936, Lincoln in 1937, and Roosevelt in 1939.

**O**f the four presidents on Mount Rushmore, Roosevelt was the one with the most significant roots in the American West. George Washington never got beyond the Ohio Valley, though it was considered the "West" of his time. Jefferson never traveled more than 70 miles west of his birthplace in Virginia. He purchased the Louisiana Territory in 1803 and sent Lewis and Clark to explore it, but he was never able to venture beyond the Appalachian Mountains. Lincoln's deepest penetration of the West was today's Nebraska. He was, in his time, regarded as a president from the West, given his birth in Kentucky and his law practice in Illinois. Lincoln also signed two pieces of key legislation in the development of the American West: the Homestead Act in 1862 and the transcontinental railroad acts in 1862 and 1864.

> *" I am proud, indeed, to be considered one of yourselves. "*
> — THEODORE ROOSEVELT

Roosevelt is the only one of the four presidents who set foot in today's South Dakota. He lived in Dakota Territory between 1883-87, invested in two badlands ranches, purchased horses in the northern Black Hills, and hunted with Deadwood Sheriff Seth Bullock.

In Dickinson, on July 4, 1886, Roosevelt was able to declare, with considerable authority, "I am, myself, at heart as much a Westerner as an Easterner; I am proud,

Roosevelt gets finishing touches at Mount Rushmore. [Jefferson at Mount Rushmore]

indeed, to be considered one of yourselves." None of the other three presidents on Mount Rushmore could honestly have made such a claim. Roosevelt not only spent time in every western state during the course of his strenuous life, but he was essentially reborn in the badlands of Dakota Territory.

Roosevelt and Borglum were friends. Borglum's bust of Abraham Lincoln, carved from a six-ton block of marble, was displayed in Roosevelt's White House before it found a permanent home in the rotunda of the U.S. Capitol.

**T**heodore Roosevelt may legitimately be regarded as the greatest and most authentically western president in American history. He was America's first cowboy president. He was also among the first privileged easterners to refashion his character and his public identity on the western frontier. During his seven-year, 171-day presidency, Roosevelt did more to promote American conservation than any president in American history.

Dakota's Mount Rushmore is a perfect site for a Roosevelt memorial, because it was here that he became the Roosevelt of American legend.

Women of the American West wait to glimpse the president.

"A vote is like a rifle: its usefulness depends upon the character of the user. The mere possession of the vote will no more benefit men and women not sufficiently developed to use it than the possession of rifles will turn untrained Egyptian fellaheen into soldiers. This is as true of woman as of man—and no more true. Universal suffrage in Hayti has not made the Haytians able to govern themselves in any true sense; and woman suffrage in Utah in no shape or way affected the problem of polygamy. I believe in suffrage for women in America, because I think they are fit for it. I believe for women, as for men, more in the duty of fitting one's self to do well and wisely with the ballot than in the naked right to cast the ballot."

*Autobiography*

# ROOSEVELT AND WOMEN

If ever there was a man's man, it was Theodore Roosevelt. If ever there was a man incapable of adultery or abusing a woman, it was Roosevelt. He imbibed a spirit of chivalry towards women from his childhood reading of dime novels and romance literature, and from his mother Mittie, a Southern belle from Roswell, Georgia.

If one were predicting Roosevelt's attitude toward women without knowing the facts of his life, it would be expected that he was a typical male chauvinist who advocated an iron wall of separation between the natural spheres of men and women.

Not so.

Roosevelt's senior essay at Harvard was entitled, "The Practicability of Equalizing Men and Women Before the Law." Historian Nathan Miller writes, "He had shown no previous interest in [women's rights] and there was no history of feminism in the Roosevelt family." In the Harvard essay Roosevelt wrote:

Even as the world is now, it is not only feasible but advisable to make women equal to men before the law. A cripple or a consumptive in the eye of the law is equal to the strongest athlete or the deepest thinker; and the same justice should be shown to a woman whether she is, or is not, the equal of man. A son should have no more right to any inheritance than a daughter should have.

He even went on to argue that a woman should not assume her husband's last name when they married. That was 1880.

During his tenure as U.S. Civil Service commissioner (1989-95), Roosevelt made it possible for women to compete on an equal basis with men for government jobs. Thanks to Roosevelt, women began their long and successful march to parity in civil service positions.

As police commissioner of New York, Roosevelt hired a woman secretary and appointed a woman to an executive position in the police department.

The legendary Jane Addams seconded Roosevelt's nomination at the Progressive (Bull Moose) Party convention in Chicago in August 1912. As a pacifist, she had serious reservations about Roosevelt's militaristic spirit. Still, she agreed with most of the Progressive Party platform and realized the importance for women of the historic role she would play at the convention. Roosevelt's Kansas friend, William Allen White, called Addams "our prize exhibit."

When Addams walked down the aisle at the convention, she received, according to White, an ovation that nearly reached the adulation accorded Roosevelt. "The Colonel was there on the platform, and I saw his eyes glisten with pride and exultant joy that she was fighting under his banner."

President Roosevelt inspects the condition of working women.

The Bull Moose Party promised the country a women's suffrage amendment. This was more than the Republican Party was willing to do. Democrat Woodrow Wilson was not even slightly in favor of women's suffrage.

For all of that, Roosevelt had a relatively traditional notion of women's role in American life—the highest and best life for women was marrying and raising republican (and Republican!) children, he reckoned. Much of Roosevelt's progressive agenda was designed to protect woman and children from strains and abuses of industrial capitalism. This made Roosevelt a paternalist as much as a feminist. He introduced a bill in New York calling for the public flogging of wife beaters.

In the long march for women's rights, Theodore Roosevelt merits historical attention as a minor, but significant, champion of equality.

> " ...it is not only feasible but advisable to make women equal to men before the law. "
> — THEODORE ROOSEVELT

The indefatigable reader, 1910.

"We have room for but one language, the language of Washington and Lincoln, the language of the Declaration of Independence and the Gettysburg speech; the English language. English should be the only language used or taught in the primary schools, public or private; in higher schools of learning other modern languages should be taught, on an equality with one another; but the language of use and instruction should be English. We should require by law that within a reasonable length of time, a time long enough to prevent needless hardship, every newspaper should be published in English. The language of the church and the Sunday-school should be English."

*The Great Adventure*

# ROOSEVELT AND THE ENGLISH LANGUAGE

Theodore Roosevelt was an incessant talker and writer. Those who loved him (and all who hated him) insisted that he was domineering at dinner parties. He lived one of the most strenuous lives in American history, yet managed to write at least 150,000 letters and several dozen books, a few of them American classics.

Depending on how you count, Roosevelt wrote more than 35 books. Although he complained of feeling awkward whenever he put pen to paper, he was a clear and unpretentious writer. His books are well written and entertaining. He exhibited a dogged self-discipline when a book deadline approached, including during the years when he was president. TR doesn't take himself too seriously in his writing. The muscularity of his prose is frequently punctuated with passages that have the feel of poetry. His letters and books about the Dakota badlands are among the best prose ever written about this region.

Roosevelt was also a phrasemaker. He is credited with giving us the phrases "lunatic fringe," "muckraker," "the man in the arena," "square deal," "malefactors of great wealth," and "good to the last drop." He also gave the popular name to the Progressive Party, thanks to his repeated references to himself "as strong as a bull moose."

He lifted a West African proverb to permanent national prominence. On September 2, 1901, he said, "There is a homely adage which runs, 'Speak softly and carry a big stick; you will go far.' If the American nation will speak softly and yet build and keep at a

Roosevelt was the readingest and writingest president in American history.

pitch of highest training a thoroughly efficient Navy, the Monroe Doctrine will go far."

> ❝ Speak softly and carry a big stick; you will go far. ❞
>
> — THEODORE ROOSEVELT

On April 15, 1906, Roosevelt coined the term "muckraker" for journalists or reformers who specialize in exposing corruption. He borrowed the term from one of his favorite books, *Pilgrim's Progress*. "Men with the muckrake," Roosevelt said, "are often indispensable to the well-being of society, but only if they know when to stop raking the muck, and to look upward to the celestial crown above them... If they

gradually grow to feel that the whole world is nothing but muck their power of usefulness is gone."

In a speech at Springfield, Illinois, in 1903, Roosevelt first uttered the phrase "square deal," which effectively became the motto of his administration. "A man who is good enough to shed his blood for his country," Roosevelt said, "is good enough to be given a square deal afterwards. More than that no man is entitled to, and less than that no man shall have."

He was also famous for pithy insults. When President McKinley hesitated to declare war on Spain after the sinking of the *Maine* (March 15, 1898), Roosevelt declared the president had the backbone of a chocolate éclair. Of another group of adversaries, he said, "You could no more make an agreement with them than you could nail currant jelly to a wall."

Roosevelt's last words were spoken to his valet, James Amos, just before his death on January 6, 1919. "Please put out the light, James."

His fair, pure, and joyous *mousekins:* Alice Hathaway Lee.

"She was beautiful in face and form, and lovelier still in spirit; as a flower she grew, and as a fair young flower she died. Her life had been always in the sunshine; and there had never come to her a single great sorrow; and none ever knew her who did not love and revere her for the bright, sunny temper and her saintly unselfishness. Fair, pure, and joyous as a maiden; loving, tender, and happy as a young wife; when she had just become a mother, when her life seemed to be but just begun, and when the years seemed so bright before her—then, by a strange and terrible fate, death came to her.

And when my heart's dearest died, the light went from my life forever."

Tribute to Alice
Summer 1884

# The Death of Roosevelt's Wife Alice

Theodore Roosevelt was married twice. His first wife Alice Hathaway Lee died on Valentine's Day 1884 at the age of 22 from complications of birthing her only child, the famous Alice Roosevelt Longworth. His second wife Edith Carow Roosevelt survived TR by 28 years. Together they had five children: Theodore, Kermit, Ethel, Archibald, and Quentin.

Roosevelt married Alice on his 22nd birthday, on October 27, 1880. She never visited Dakota Territory. He was helplessly in love with her and called her by such names as "mousekins," "my sunny faced darling," and "my little witch of a sweetheart."

Roosevelt was attending to legislative duties in Albany, New York, when word came that Alice had given birth a little prematurely on February 12, 1884. The following day he received a second telegram informing him that Alice was dying. He rushed back to their New York City home, arriving late on February 13. His brother Elliott was waiting at the door. "There is a curse on this house," Elliott said, for not only was Alice dying of Bright's disease, a total collapse of her kidney function, but Roosevelt's mother Mittie was dying in the same house on the same night of typhoid fever. She was 49 years old.

Mittie Roosevelt died in the early morning hours of February 14, 1884. Alice died a few hours later. In short, the two most important women in Theodore Roosevelt's life died simultaneously in the same house on Valentine's Day 1884.

> " The light has gone out of my life. "
>
> — Theodore Roosevelt

In his pocket diary for Valentine's Day Roosevelt drew a large X, and wrote, "The light has gone out of my life."

After the double funeral he returned to Albany, wrapped up his legislative responsibilities, then attended the 1884 Republican National Convention in Chicago, where he and reformist friends, including Henry Cabot Lodge, watched helplessly as a corrupt man was nominated for the presidency.

Then TR returned to the badlands of Dakota Territory to nurse his grief and bury himself in frontier life. He was certain he would never get over his loss and actually contemplated spending the rest of his life in the West. Roosevelt threw

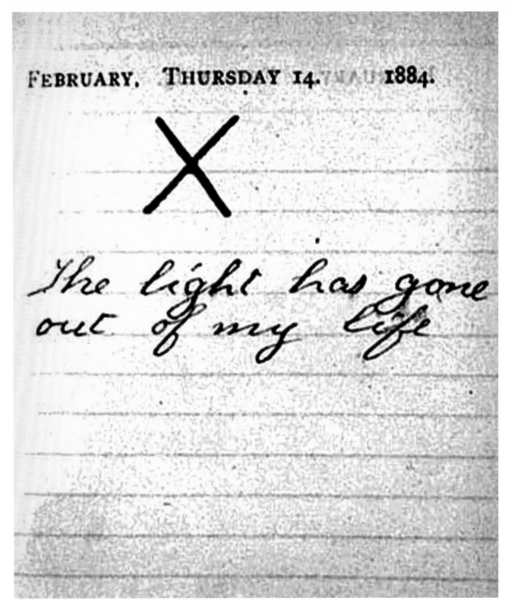

Roosevelt's pocket diary from the fatal day in 1884.

himself into hard work and adventure, pressing the "strenuous life" at times into the realm of recklessness.

Roosevelt recovered his spirit in the Dakota badlands after long solo rides in an open faraway country. With great personal insight he later wrote, "Black care seldom sits behind a rider whose pace is fast enough."

For the rest of his life, Roosevelt refused to mention his first wife—even to his curious and needy child Alice. He tended to call his illustrious daughter Sister or Baby Lee to avoid mentioning the name of his lost first love. In his 1913 *Autobiography*, among the best in presidential history, Roosevelt did not once mention his first marriage. Nor did he like to be called Teddy (though everyone did), because that had been Alice's pet name for her adoring husband.

Roosevelt's extraordinary second wife Edith, who had strengths of mind and character that his first wife never exhibited, later said, a little sharply, that TR would have died of boredom had Alice Hathaway Lee lived.

The presidential pugilist in the arena: *Puck* magazine, July 20, 1904.

"I wish to preach, not the doctrine of ignoble ease, but the doctrine of the strenuous life, the life of toil and effort, of labor and strife; to preach that highest form of success which comes, not to the man who desires mere easy peace, but to the man who does not shrink from danger, from hardship, or from bitter toil, and to who out of these wins the splendid ultimate triumph."

*The Strenuous Life*

# A Strenuous Life of Bodily Injury

In fall 1885, Theodore Roosevelt broke his arm during Long Island's Meadowbrook Hunt. He was attempting to jump a wall when his exhausted stallion tripped. Roosevelt's face was badly cut and his left arm snapped beneath the elbow, but he got back on the horse and continued the hunt.

Afterwards he wrote, "I don't grudge the broken arm a bit... I'm always ready to pay the piper when I've had a good dance; and every now and then I like to drink the wine of life with brandy in it."

This was essentially Roosevelt's philosophy of life.

It would be impossible to tally all of the broken bones, cuts, abrasions, and other injuries Roosevelt endured in his hectic life of 60 years.

During his time in Dakota Territory, Roosevelt was frequently thrown from horses. On one occasion, his horse fell over backwards on him, cracking the point of his left shoulder. Since there was no doctor nearby, Roosevelt let the injury heal itself. On a buffalo hunt in 1883, Roosevelt's horse—spooked by a buffalo—reared back so suddenly that TR's rifle knocked him sharply on the forehead. He bled, according to his guide Joe Ferris, like a stuck pig, but did not stop the hunt.

In the summer of 1892, Roosevelt was climbing a windmill at Sagamore Hill when a blade gashed him in the forehead. He bled profusely and rushed into the house. His wife Edith looked up and nonchalantly ordered TR to go take care of himself in the bathroom. She did not want him bleeding on the rug.

Roosevelt was always ready to pay the piper. He often did.

> **"I'm always ready to pay the piper when I've had a good dance."**
>
> — Theodore Roosevelt

On September 3, 1902, Roosevelt was traveling from Pittsfield to Lenox, Massachusetts. As the presidential carriage crossed tracks that were supposed to have been cleared, a loaded trolley slammed into the carriage, throwing the president and his secretary 30 feet, and instantly killing Secret Service agent William Craig. Roosevelt suffered cuts, bruises, and a leg injury that plagued him for the rest of his life. Roosevelt was more concerned about Craig's death than his own injuries. "Too bad, too bad," he said. "Poor Craig. How my children will feel!"

Roosevelt tried to stay in shape during his presidential years by boxing. During a match with a young military officer in 1904, Roosevelt insisted that his opponent not hold back. The officer promptly popped the president in the left eye, blinding Roosevelt in that eye for the rest of his life. The press was not informed, partly as a courtesy to the officer, whom TR did not blame for the injury.

Roosevelt's greatest injury came by way of an assassin's bullet. While campaigning in Milwaukee on October 14, 1912, saloon keeper John Schrank shot him at point blank range. "He pinked me," said Roosevelt, who instantly recognized that he was seriously, but not mortally wounded. Roosevelt determined to give his scheduled speech anyway. "This is my big chance," he said, "and I am going to make that speech if I die doing it."

Roosevelt gave an 84-minute speech before his handlers took him to a hospital. "It takes more than that," he crowed, "to kill a Bull Moose."

Cowboys at the Elkhorn Ranch, 1919.

"Nowhere, not even at sea, does a man feel more lonely than when riding over the far-reaching, seemingly never-ending plains; and after a man has lived a little while on or near them, their very vastness and loneliness and their melancholy monotony have a strong fascination for him. The landscape seems always the same, and after the traveler has plodded on for miles and miles he gets to feel as if the distance was indeed boundless. As far as the eye can see there is no break; either the prairie stretches out into perfectly level flats, or else there are gentle, rolling slopes, whose crests mark the divide between the drainage systems of the different creeks; and when one of these is ascended, immediately another precisely like it takes its place in the distance, and so roll succeeds roll in a succession as interminable as that of the waves of the ocean."

*Hunting Trips of a Ranchman*

# THEODORE ROOSEVELT AND NORTH DAKOTA

Theodore Roosevelt first came to Dakota Territory in September 1883 to hunt buffalo. He immediately fell in love with the badlands and the Little Missouri River Valley. He established two ranches in the badlands—the Maltese Cross and the Elkhorn. From 1883-87, he spent a significant amount of time hunting, writing, riding, seeking adventure, and raising cattle in Dakota Territory.

Roosevelt's Dakota experiences transformed him from a class-conscious New York dude into America's greatest exemplar of the strenuous life. He also gained a new appreciation for the colorful, hard-working people of the American heartland. He would become their advocate in his call for a Square Deal for all American citizens.

At one point, after the death of his first wife Alice, Roosevelt thought he might spend the rest of his life in the West. He toyed with the idea of becoming one of the region's first senators when statehood came. In 1885, however, he fell in love with his childhood sweetheart Edith Carow in New York. They were married in London, England, on December 2, 1886. Thereafter, Roosevelt regarded his Dakota ranches more as hunting lodges than as his true home.

North Dakota became a state on November 2, 1889. By then most of Roosevelt's adventures in the badlands were over.

Thanks to his experiences in the badlands, for the rest of his life Roosevelt was more often depicted as a cowboy than in any other of his many guises. He was the first urban president to get a transfusion of political appeal and mythic status from a sojourn in the American West. TR was the first president to be the constant subject of political cartoons. Whenever he did something hectic or impulsive (which was virtually every day), he was depicted wearing a cowboy hat, boots, spurs, and a pistol. When he became president in September 1901, one detractor, Senator Mark Hanna of Ohio, said, "Now look, that damned cowboy is President of the United States."

Roosevelt wrote three books about his experiences in the Dakota badlands and never tired of talking about his frontier adventures. He also devoted one of the finest chapters in his 1913 *Autobiography* to his time "In Cowboy Land." Although he

> " It was here that the romance of my life began. "
> — THEODORE ROOSEVELT

Roosevelt came to North Dakota loaded for bear – or elk or antelope or bighorn sheep.

frequently exaggerated the amount of time he actually spent in North Dakota, it would have been impossible for Roosevelt to exaggerate the effect it had on his soul. In 1910, dedicating a library in Fargo, ND, Roosevelt said, "I never would have been President if it had not been for my experiences in North Dakota."

In 1904 Roosevelt had an intriguing conversation with Senator Albert Fall of New Mexico: "Do you know what chapter in all my life... looking back over all of it... I would choose to remember, were the alternative forced upon me to recall one portion of it, and to have erased from my memory all other experiences? I would take the memory of my life on the ranch with its experiences close to nature and among the men who lived nearest her." That must be regarded as Roosevelt's definitive endorsement of the significance of his time in Dakota Territory.

And in 1900, visiting Medora during a campaign swing for President McKinley, Roosevelt said it best: "It was here that the romance of my life began."

Stalwarts of the Dakota badlands in the time of Roosevelt's adventures.

"Out on the frontier, and generally among those who spend their lives in, or on the borders of the wilderness, life is reduced to its elemental conditions. The passions and emotions of these grim hunters of the mountains, and wild rough-riders of the plains, are simpler and stronger than those of people dwelling in more complicated states of society. As soon as the communities become settled and begin to grow with any rapidity, the American instinct for law asserts itself; but in the earlier stages each individual is obliged to be a law to himself and to guard his rights with a strong hand. Of course the transition periods are full of incongruities. Men have not yet adjusted their relations to morality and law with any niceness… Unfortunately in the far West the transition takes place at an altogether unheard-of speed, and many a man's nature is unable to change with sufficient rapidity to allow him to harmonize with his environment. In consequence, unless he leaves for still wilder lands, he ends by getting hanged instead of founding a family."

*The Wilderness Hunter*

# WHAT ROOSEVELT SOUGHT IN DAKOTA TERRITORY

Theodore Roosevelt came to the badlands of Dakota Territory in September 1883 to hunt a buffalo. He fell in love with this region of lonely buttes and stark broken country, invested in two badlands ranches, and spent the better part of four years hunting, riding, and ranching on the frontier.

What was he seeking in the west?

First, like many wealthy men from the East Coast and Europe, he saw himself as an investor in the cattle industry. Much had been published about the economic potential of the northern Great Plains, particularly the "badlands country" of North Dakota, Montana, and Wyoming. Even before he came to the Dakota badlands, Roosevelt had invested $10,000 in a cattle ranch in Wyoming.

Roosevelt would eventually invest approximately $82,500 in his two North Dakota ranches. His uncle James Roosevelt, who managed his finances, regarded his frontier investments as foolhardy. From a financial perspective, Uncle James was right. Roosevelt lost approximately $23,500 between 1883-87, a significant percentage of his net worth. He never regretted it for a moment!

Second, Roosevelt wanted a place to hunt. Big game hunting was one of the central interests of his life. In Dakota Territory, Roosevelt bagged at least one of each of the major quadrupeds: buffalo, mule deer, white tail deer, bighorn sheep, elk, and pronghorn antelope. Even after he cut his losses and withdrew from the cattle industry (ca. 1898), Roosevelt continued to regard the Elkhorn Ranch cabin as his primary western hunting lodge.

Third, after Valentine's Day 1884 he needed a place to grieve in solitude for his first wife Alice, who died just two days after giving birth to her only child, the famous Alice Roosevelt Longworth. In June 1884, Roosevelt created a second badlands ranch, the Elkhorn, 35 miles north of Medora, to get away from the press of visitors at the Maltese Cross Ranch, seven miles south of Medora. Even today, the Elkhorn Ranch is sufficiently remote to be seldom visited.

Fourth, Roosevelt wanted to drink in American frontier life before it disappeared forever. TR knew the

> *(Roosevelt) himself realized what a splendid thing it was for him to have been here at that time and to have had sufficient strength in his character to absorb it.*
>
> — DR. VICTOR HUGO STICKNEY

Roosevelt reading and roughing it in the American West.

frontier phase of American history was coming to an end. He wanted the opportunity to share something of the experience of his heroes George Rogers Clark, Daniel Boone, and Davy Crockett before it was too late. If it was the frontier that had made America great, and there was still a sliver of it on the western edge of Dakota Territory, Roosevelt was determined to extract whatever that disappearing frontier had to offer, and to incorporate it into his own character.

Roosevelt's friend Dr. Victor Hugo Stickney of Dickinson later said, "It was a wonderful thing for Roosevelt. He himself realized what a splendid thing it was for him to have been here at that time and to have had sufficient strength in his character to absorb it. He started out to get the fundamental truths as they were in this country and he never lost sight of that purpose all the time he was here."

It was this infusion of "frontier dynamics" that led Roosevelt to say, for the rest of his life, "I never would have been President if it had not been for my experiences in North Dakota."

The whilom dude in his rough and easy costume.

September 8, 1883

Darling Wifie,

Yesterday evening I took the six o'clock train from Bismarck, and sat up till ten playing whist with a party of jolly young englishmen. Then I tumbled into my bunk and at two o'clock tumbled out, at Little Missouri Station. It was bitterly cold, and it was some time before, groping about among the four or five shanties which formed the "town," I found the low, small building called the "hotel." There were no lights, but vigorous pounding on the door at last awakened the cursing landlord; he showed me up the un-railed stairs to the second story, which was not divided into rooms at all, but was simply a long, bare garret, with eight or ten beds, most of them with sleepers who greeted my advent with anything but cordiality; but, cold and sleepy, I paid them small heed, turned promptly into a vacant bed and slept soundly till morning. At breakfast (before which we all washed in the same tin basin) I met Gorringe's secretary, Mr. U. R. Wright, a wide awake Yankee, who received me with the greatest cordiality, and got me to at once shift my things over to the Company's ranch building, where I have a room to myself and am very comfortable."

Roosevelt's first letter from Dakota Territory
To his wife Alice Lee Roosevelt
September 8, 1883

# ROOSEVELT ARRIVES IN THE BADLANDS

Theodore Roosevelt was just 24 years old when he stepped off the train in Little Missouri, the tiny frontier village just across the Little Missouri River from Medora, on the night of September 7-8, 1883. The frail New York reformer and state assemblyman had ventured west on the Northern Pacific Railroad to hunt a buffalo.

His life would never be the same.

Roosevelt arrived in the Dakota badlands in the dark, after a five-day journey from New York. It was 3 a.m. by the time he exited the train. All the territory was asleep. Medora did not yet exist and the raw little village of Little Missouri had neither depot nor train platform to greet the New York reformer and assemblyman. Theodore Roosevelt was on his own in one of the last frontiers of the American West. His friend H.H. Gorringe had convinced him that the Dakota badlands were the place to bag one of the last buffalo on the North American continent.

In 1883 Roosevelt was just three years out of Harvard and married for just under three years. He was the youngest member of the New York State Assembly, already known as an uncompromising political reformer. He had been to today's North Dakota just once before, in 1880, and then only a few miles west of the Red River near Moorhead, Minnesota. At the time of his arrival in the badlands, Roosevelt was a lean, frail, class-conscious New Yorker who wore spectacles and spoke in a reedy falsetto. People said he bit off his words with the snap of his oversize teeth. He was, in 1883, decidedly not the sort of man likely to win the respect and affection of the hard-boiled men of the Dakota frontier.

The weary Roosevelt carried his bag a few hundred feet north to the Pyramid Park Hotel, where after furious knocking, he managed to rouse the grumpy proprietor, Frank Moore. There were no available private rooms in the inn.

> *" It was here that the romance of my life began. "*
> — THEODORE ROOSEVELT

The *luxurious* Pyramid Park Hotel (on the right) in its heyday.

"Captain Moore" told Roosevelt that for 25 cents he could have the last of 10 cots upstairs in an open-air loft called the "bullpen." The New York dude tender-footed his way through a baker's dozen of snoring and unsympathetic frontiersmen to the sole available cot in the room. He slept surprisingly well.

At dawn, a bell rang to announce breakfast. Roosevelt said the rough men of the bunkhouse "stampeded" down the wooden stairs to get to the grub. The fastidious Roosevelt wanted to wash up before breakfast. The basin of water in the common area and the sole towel were as foul as anything he had ever seen, but he cheerfully realized that he was not in New York anymore, and he soon discovered that his appetite was "by no means impaired."

After breakfast, Roosevelt took a brisk walk through the nearby badlands. He had been cooped up on the train for days. He wanted to see the lay of the land and to breathe in the crisp, dry air of the American West. Then he started looking for a local guide to take him to the nearest buffalo.

Years later he would say, "It was here that the romance of my life began."

Joe Ferris: "Bad luck followed us like a yellow dog follows a drunkard."

"The buffalo is more easily killed than any other kind of plains game; but its chase is very far from being the tame amusement it has lately been represented. It is genuine sport; it needs skill, marksmanship, and hardihood in the man who follows it, and if he hunts on horseback, it needs also pluck and good riding. It is in no way akin to various forms of so-called sport in vogue in parts of the East, such as killing deer in a lake or by fire-hunting, or even by watching at a runway. No man who is not of an adventurous temper, and able to stand rough food and living, will penetrate to the haunts of the buffalo. The animal is so tough and tenacious of life that it must be hit in the right spot; and care must be used in approaching it, for its nose is very keen."

*Hunting Trips of a Ranchman*

# IT BEGAN WITH A BUFFALO HUNT

Theodore Roosevelt came to Dakota Territory in September 1883 for one purpose—to kill a buffalo. He got his buffalo after a 14-day hunt that was something of an ordeal. In the course of that adventure, however, he fell in love with the Dakota badlands.

After arriving by train in the middle of the night and catching a few hours of sleep at the Pyramid Park Hotel (long gone) in the now-abandoned village of Little Missouri, Roosevelt took a long walk to inspect the badlands, which he was seeing for the first time.

He hired a reluctant guide—Joe Ferris—who later became one of his best Dakota friends. He borrowed a gun from a rough local hunter by the name of E.G. Paddock, who had a habit of making his enemies disappear. He bought a horse because the local folks didn't yet trust him or like him enough to lend him one. Roosevelt and Ferris spent their first night at the Maltese Cross Ranch seven miles south of Medora. Roosevelt was so impressed with the badlands country that he bought the ranch on September 20, 1883, just before returning by train to New York.

By the fall of 1883 most of the buffalo of the American West were gone—victims of hide hunters and a deliberate national policy of eliminating the foundation of the American Indian lifeway. Once numbering in the tens of millions, perhaps only a few hundred of the great creatures still grazed the plains by 1883. Roosevelt actually believed that the buffalo would become extinct. He wanted to get one first! But

The American bison: from 60 million to a few hundred in half a century.

he later went on to play an important role in the saving of the buffalo from extinction and their slow recovery in such National Parks as Wind Cave and Yellowstone and at several National Bison Ranges.

> *Bad luck followed us like a yellow dog follows a drunkard.*
>
> — JOE FERRIS

Roosevelt had a very hard time finding a buffalo to kill in September 1883. The buffalo he and Ferris saw near Marmarth, ND, and Pretty Butte eluded them, partly because Roosevelt was too excited to shoot straight, partly because they had a string of really bad luck, including drizzly weather. At one point when Roosevelt thought he was about to shoot his buffalo, the horse he was on reared up and TR's gun barrel struck him in the forehead. He bled, he said, like a stuck pig. On another occasion, inching towards a buffalo on

his hands and knees, Roosevelt crawled straight into a prickly pear cactus patch.

"Bad luck followed us," Ferris later said, "like a yellow dog follows a drunkard."

Finally, on September 16, just west of the Montana line near the source of Little Cannonball Creek, Roosevelt shot his first buffalo. It struggled up over a ridge. When he and Ferris reached the spot where the great quadruped finally fell, Roosevelt spontaneously did a little "Indian war dance" around the carcass and impulsively pulled out a $100 bill to give to Ferris.

A day or two later he removed the head of the great creature, transported it back to New York, and proudly displayed it for the rest of his life in the North Room at his Sagamore Hill home. It can be seen there today.

Medora as Roosevelt knew it, ca. 1885.

"We speak of it as an antelope, and it does of course represent on our prairies the antelopes of the Old World; but it stands apart from all other horned animals. Its place in the natural world is almost as lonely as that of the giraffe. In all its ways and habits it differs as much from deer and elk as from goat and sheep. Now that the buffalo has gone, it is the only game really at home on the wide plains. It is a striking-looking little creature, with its prominent eyes, single-pronged horns, and the sharply contrasted white, brown, and reddish of its coat… In marked contrast to deer, antelope never seek to elude observation; all they care for is to be able themselves to see."

*Outdoor Pastimes of an American Hunter*

# ROOSEVELT AND LINCOLN LANG

Lincoln Lang and his father Gregor Lang settled in the Dakota badlands just a few months before Theodore Roosevelt arrived for his buffalo hunt in 1883. Sent by British industrialist Sir John Pender (the creator of the first successful Atlantic cable), Gregor Lang established a ranch approximately 50 miles south of Medora at the mouth of Little Cannonball Creek.

Gregor was an enterprising and politically astute man from Scotland, who—against strong family protests—named his son Lincoln, after the Great Emancipator Abraham Lincoln.

Roosevelt appeared at the Lang ranch near Pretty Butte at dusk on the night of September 9, 1883. He was on horseback. His guide Joe Ferris was driving a buckboard. In the way of western hospitality, Gregor offered them food and a place to stay, and it was soon determined that Ferris and Roosevelt would use the Lang cabin as their "headquarters" for the buffalo hunt. Roosevelt absolutely refused to take one of the beds in the crude cabin. He found a place on the dirt floor to throw down his blanket.

Lincoln Lang was just 14 years old at the time. In 1926 he wrote a remarkable account of his years in the badlands, *Ranching with Roosevelt.* It is the source for much of what we know about TR's time in Dakota Territory.

Lincoln never forgot that first meeting. Gregor Lang said, "This is my son Lincoln, Mr. Roosevelt."

"Dee-lighted to meet you, Lincoln."

Lincoln immediately recognized two things. First, Roosevelt was genuinely dee-lighted. He was incapable of posturing. Second, "Certain it is, right there and then, I fell for him strong."

Each morning at dawn, Roosevelt and his reluctant guide Joe Ferris ventured out in search of a buffalo. Each night they returned empty-handed, exhausted, and covered with mud. It drizzled through most of the 10 days Roosevelt spent with the Langs, and everyone tried to talk him out of hunting in the rain and gumbo. But there was no stopping him.

After supper each night, Ferris went straight to bed. Roosevelt, after a day of exhaustion and frustration, wanted to stay up to talk with Gregor, whose strong convictions about democracy and reform were similar to Roosevelt's. Lincoln Lang remembered listening to their spirited and idealistic talk deep into the nights.

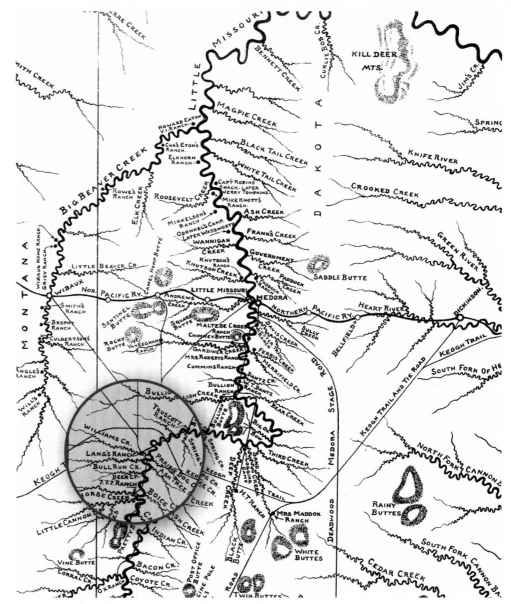

The Gregor and Lincoln Lang Ranch near today's Marmarth, ND.

When Roosevelt finally got his buffalo, he brought back rump roasts to share with the Langs. Then, after removing the head of the buffalo for later display at his home on Long Island, Roosevelt bid the Langs temporary farewell.

Gregor said, "There goes the most remarkable man I ever met."

> *There goes the most remarkable man I ever met.*
> — GREGOR LANG

Lincoln did better than that. Years later he recalled, "It was in listening to those talks after supper in the old shack on the Cannonball that I first came to understand that the Lord made the earth for all of us and not for a chosen few."

Alden Eaten of the Custer Trail Ranch in an *authentic buckskin shirt.*

"The old race of Rocky Mountain hunters and trappers, of reckless, dauntless Indian fighters, is now fast dying out. Yet here and there these restless wanderers of the untrodden wilderness still linger in wooded fastnesses so inaccessible that the miners have not yet explored them, in mountain valleys so far out that no ranchman has yet driven his herds thither. To this day many of them wear the fringed tunic or hunting-shirt, made of buckskin or homespun, and belted in at the waist—the most picturesque and distinctively national dress ever worn in America."

*Ranch Life and the Hunting Trail*

# ROOSEVELT AND THE AUTHENTIC BUCKSKIN SHIRT

Theodore Roosevelt fell in love with the Dakota badlands during his sojourn in Dakota Territory between 1883 and 1887. He invested in two area ranches in an attempt to experience fully American frontier life before it disappeared forever. During one visit in 1884, Roosevelt journeyed down to Gregor and Lincoln Lang's cabin between Bullion and Pretty Buttes, about 50 miles south of Medora. He wanted Gregor Lang to help him draw up a contract to buy 1,000 more head of cattle for his Maltese Cross Ranch.

Roosevelt wanted desperately to be an "authentic" cowboy. He was a friend to Frederic Remington and Owen Wister, and he greatly admired such genuine westerners as Seth Bullock, the sheriff of Deadwood, and Buckey O'Neil, the Arizona Rough Rider who died in Cuba in 1898. Roosevelt wanted to drink in every possible frontier experience. He did not want to look like an outsider *playing* a cowboy, but rather to be a *cowboy* who also had a life back east.

Roosevelt recruited Gregor's son Lincoln for a grand adventure. "Lincoln, there are two things I want to do. I want to get an antelope, and I want to get a buckskin shirt." The antelope made perfect sense. Roosevelt was a serious hunter. It was his intention to kill at least one of every significant game species available in the badlands.

It was the shirt that required explanation. According to Roosevelt's theory of the American West, "The fringed tunic or hunting shirt made of buckskin [represented] the most picturesque and distinctly national dress ever worn in America. It was the dress in which Daniel Boone was clad when he first passed through the trackless forests of the Alleghenies… it was the dress worn by grim old Davy Crockett when he fell at the Alamo." Because he wanted desperately to be

> *" I want to get an antelope, and I want to get a buckskin shirt. "*
>
> — THEODORE ROOSEVELT

Roosevelt in his famous buckskin shirt, photographed in New York City during the badlands years.

an authentic frontiersman, Roosevelt felt that he must have such a shirt.

Lincoln reckoned they could meet both goals in a daylong horseback trip east of the badlands. A Mrs. Maddox had a cabin 20 miles east on Sand Creek near the old Keogh Trail. She was known to be a tough, no-nonsense, hard-swearing woman who had recently chased her no-good husband off the property with a stove lid lifter.

So Roosevelt and Lincoln set out on a June day in 1884. They spent an agreeable evening with Mrs. Maddox, who served them a good dinner, entertained (and slightly awed) Roosevelt, and measured the New York dude for his "authentic" buckskin shirt. Lang later wrote, "Almost at once, she seemed to take a liking to Roosevelt, becoming quite chatty, which was unusual for her with strangers." Whether Roosevelt explained to Mrs. Maddox his theory of the buckskin shirt is unknown. If he did, it is a pity that Lincoln Lang did not record her reaction!

On the return journey, Roosevelt shot his first pronghorn antelope. A few weeks later he got the quintessential American tunic. That shirt remained in the Roosevelt family for decades.

E.G. Paddock lived in a shack on the lower right.

"There were bad characters in the Western country at that time, of course, and under the conditions of life they were probably more dangerous than they would have been elsewhere. I hardly ever had any difficulty, however. I never went into a saloon, and in the little hotels I kept out of the barroom unless, as sometimes happened, the barroom was the only room on the lower floor except the dining-room. I always endeavored to keep out of a quarrel until self-respect forbade my making any further effort to avoid it, and I very rarely had even the semblance of trouble."

*Autobiography*

# ROOSEVELT AND E.G. PADDOCK

E. G. (Gerry) Paddock was one of the notorious personalities of the badlands during Theodore Roosevelt's 1883-87 sojourn in Dakota Territory. He was one of the original hunters in the region and a guide for wealthy greenhorns who ventured to the Dakota badlands for sport. Paddock was a lethal man in a quarrel. His enemies had been known to suffer mysterious accidents or to disappear altogether. He was never a man to be trifled with.

When Roosevelt first came to the badlands in September 1883 to hunt a buffalo, he discovered that the Winchester rifle he had brought from New York had a broken hammer. Roosevelt's guide Joe Ferris suggested that Paddock might let Roosevelt borrow a more appropriate firearm. The pair rode to Paddock's shack. Paddock sized TR up and immediately lent him a better buffalo gun.

By the time Roosevelt returned to the badlands in 1884, Paddock had aligned himself with French nobleman and entrepreneur the Marquis de Mores. The presence of de Mores had split the badlands community into two factions—those who had an almost feudal dependency on the Marquis, and those who disliked his manner and worked hard to maintain their independence. Roosevelt's closest friends in Dakota—Gregor and Lincoln Lang, Joe and Sylvane Ferris, and Bill Merrifield—belonged to the anti-de Mores faction.

The lordly Marquis de Mores regarded the entire Little Missouri River Valley as his private domain. He bought up land at a time when the badlands were still being grazed by squatter's law. Worse than that, he fenced the open range—a form of heresy that appalled everyone not in de Mores' employ and led to a shoot out in which the Marquis and his henchmen killed a young man named Riley Luffsey. Paddock was de Mores' right hand man and his "enforcer."

> " I have come over to see when you want to begin the killing... "
>
> — THEODORE ROOSEVELT

The Marquis let Roosevelt know he regarded the Elkhorn bottom (35 miles north of Medora) as his own, that he had prior grazing claim to the site Roosevelt chose for his second ranch. Roosevelt dismissed the Marquis' claim with a shrug. Paddock, on de Mores' behalf, insisted he had a prior squatter's claim to

Roosevelt would not let himself be bullied even by a man known for making his enemies disappear.

the Elkhorn. Finally, Paddock let Roosevelt's ranch hands know that he was going to shoot Roosevelt at the next opportunity.

Roosevelt saddled his horse. He rode to Medora and made his way quietly to Paddock's shack on the west bank of the Little Missouri River. He got off his horse and knocked on Paddock's door.

"Paddock. I understand that you have threatened to kill me on sight. I have come over to see when you want to begin the killing and to let you know that, if you have anything to say against me, now is the time for you to say it."

Probably Paddock had never seen such fearlessness in the whole course of his life. Paddock assured Roosevelt that he had been "misquoted," that he had no intention of shooting Roosevelt, that he had no fundamental disagreement with Roosevelt, and he would quite like to maintain cordial relations with Roosevelt.

That was the end of that.

Roosevelt's friends in 1919: Joe Ferris, Sylvane Ferris, Bill Merrifield.

"My own experience was that if a man did not talk until his associates knew him well and liked him, and if he did his work, he never had any difficulty in getting on. In my own round-up district I speedily grew to be friends with most of the men. When I went among strangers I always had to spend twenty-four hours in living down the fact that I wore spectacles, remaining as long as I could judiciously, deaf to any side remarks about 'four eyes,' unless it became evident that my being quiet was misconstrued and that it was better to bring matters to a head at once."

*Autobiography*

# HOW THE NATIVES SAW ROOSEVELT

For a long time they regarded him as a New York dude, a punkinlilly, an interloper. It didn't help that he "spoke funny" with an aristocratic Harvard falsetto. It didn't help that he wore silver spurs with his initials on them and a knife hand-carved by Tiffany's. It didn't help that he wore thick glasses.

"When I went among strangers," Roosevelt later wrote, "I always had to spend twenty-four hours in living down the fact that I wore spectacles, remaining as long as I could judiciously deaf to any side remarks about 'four eyes' unless it became evident that my being quiet was misconstrued and that it was better to bring matters to a head at once."

Local badlands folks had seen dudes come and go before. Their general approach was to be friendly in a skeptical way, to take some of the dudes' money if possible, and to remember that these highfalutin visitors were likely to disappear as quickly as they appeared on the scene.

Local hunting guide Joe Ferris had been reluctant to take the urban New Yorker buffalo hunting. He expected Roosevelt to give up his quest after a couple of days wandering in the drizzle and gumbo of the Dakota badlands. When Ferris discovered that Roosevelt was uncomplaining, dogged, and cheerful even in the most provoking field circumstances, he gained a lifelong respect for TR. "He could stand an awful lot of hard knocks," Ferris later recalled. "You just couldn't knock him out of sorts. He was entertaining, too, and I liked to listen to him, though, on the whole, he wasn't much on the talk. He said that he wanted to get away from politics, so I didn't mention political matters; and he had books with him and would read at odd times."

> " There goes the most remarkable man I ever met. "
>
> — GREGOR LANG

Badlands rancher Frank Roberts recalled, "He was rather a slim-lookin' fellow when he came out here, but after he lived out here . . . his build got wider and heavier . . . he got to be lookin' more like a rugged man."

Dutch Wannigan was one of the survivors of the Riley Luffsey shooting in 1883. This photograph was taken in 1919.

Scottish immigrant Gregor Lang shared Roosevelt's love of Abraham Lincoln, American democracy, and political reform, though they belonged to opposite political parties. When Roosevelt left the Lang ranch after using it as the headquarters for his buffalo hunt, Lang told his son Lincoln, "There goes the most remarkable man I ever met."

Roosevelt's body and soul underwent a transformation in the Dakota badlands. The *St. Paul Pioneer Press* noticed. "Rugged, bronzed, and in the prime of health, Theodore Roosevelt passed through St. Paul yesterday, returning from his Dakota ranch to New York and civilization. There was very little of the whilom dude in his rough and easy costume, with a large handkerchief tied loosely about his neck; but the eyeglasses and the flashing eyes behind them, the pleasant smile and hearty grasp of hand remained."

Roosevelt never won the hearts and minds of every Dakotan, then or now. But most people he encountered in his badlands sojourn recognized his passion and his authenticity, and most—like Joe Ferris and Gregor Lang—gained a lifelong admiration that bordered on reverence.

Roosevelt knew that the cowboy phase of western history would be temporary.

"It is the life of men who live in the open, who tend their herds on horseback, who go armed and ready to guard their lives by their own prowess, whose wants are very simple, and who call no man master. Ranching is an occupation like those of vigorous, primitive pastoral peoples, having little in common with the humdrum, workaday business world of the nineteenth century; and the free ranchman in his manner of life shows more kinship to an Arab sheik than to a sleek city merchant or tradesman."

*Ranch Life and the Hunting Trail*

# ROOSEVELT AND THE GRAZING ASSOCIATION

Several men had attempted to organize cattleman of the Little Missouri River Valley before Theodore Roosevelt got involved. But he was the one who made it happen.

Theodore Roosevelt was a born leader.

The need for a stockman's association was acknowledged by nearly every law-abiding rancher in the badlands. Horse thieves were working eastern Montana and western Dakota Territory virtually unmolested. Because there were few fences, and herds from up and down the valley mingled indiscriminately, close cooperation was essential during the twice-annual roundup to sort out and return everyone's stray cattle. The casual system of siting ranches and defining grazing rights inevitably led to conflict. Some agreement about what constituted over-grazing needed to be reached— and then enforced. Billings County was not formally organized until 1886. The nearest United States Marshal was 200 miles south at Deadwood. The nearest sheriff was in Mandan, 130 miles east.

Roosevelt called a meeting of interested ranchers for December 19, 1884. Between November 16, when he arrived at Medora, and the date of the meeting, Roosevelt rode up and down the Little Missouri River urging ranchers to participate in the proposed organization.

> " ...if he had shot me down he knew he could not have escaped swift retribution."
>
> — THEODORE ROOSEVELT

Grazers of the upper Great Plains in the era of Roosevelt.

The meeting became the stuff of legend. About a dozen ranchers or their representatives attended. A number of others sent letters endorsing the goals of the proposed organization. Roosevelt was elected chairman of the meeting, a considerable honor for a man who was a novice cattleman and an outsider in so many ways.

Some sort of confrontation occurred at that Medora meeting. Deputy Marshal Fred A. Willard, a man who hid behind rather than exemplified the badge he wore, attempted to disrupt the meeting. He represented those who firmly opposed the idea of a grazing association. Accounts disagree about exactly what happened. At the very least, sharp words were exchanged between Willard and Roosevelt. According to one account, Willard drew his pistol and held it against TR's stomach. Roosevelt shouted, "Shoot and be damned... you pledged your honor to uphold the laws of the United States and you are in league with the lawbreakers... Get out!"

Other eyewitnesses disputed the notion that guns were actually drawn, but they all acknowledged that Roosevelt refused to be bullied and succeeded in pushing Willard out the door. Years later, Roosevelt said, "There was no other way, and it had exactly the effect we desired. I do not think I was in any danger. I was unarmed, and if he had shot me down he knew he could not have escaped swift retribution. Besides, I was right, and he knew it!"

The meeting accomplished its goals. Seven resolutions were passed, one of which empowered Roosevelt to write bylaws for the grazing association. The Marquis de Mores, a local French land baron and entrepreneur, was appointed to work with the eastern Montana grazing association to promote laws favorable to the cattle industry. The organization decided to call itself the Little Missouri River Stockmen's Association.

Probably there would still have been a grazing association if Roosevelt had never visited the badlands. But his role in its creation was characteristic of his leadership capacities, his love of law and order, and his understanding that such voluntary associations represented an important tradition in the frontier's development of self-government.

"There were monotonous days, as we guided the trail cattle."

"One night there was a heavy storm, and all of us who were at the wagons were obliged to turn out hastily to help the night herders. After a while there was a terrific peal of thunder, the lightning struck right by the herd, and away all the beasts went, heads and horns and tails in the air. For a minute or two I could make out nothing except the dark forms of the beasts running on every side of me, and I should have been very sorry if my horses had stumbled, for those behind me would have trodden me down. Then the herd split, part going to one side, while the other part seemingly kept straight ahead, and I galloped as hard as ever beside them. I was trying to reach the point—the leading animals—in order to turn them, when suddenly there was a tremendous splashing in front. I could dimly make out that the cattle immediately ahead and to one side of me were disappearing, and the next moment the horse and I went off a cut bank into the Little Missouri. I bent away back in the saddle, and though the horse almost went down, he just recovered himself, and, plunging and struggling through water and quicksand, we made the other side."

*Autobiography*

# ROOSEVELT GETS HIS STAMPEDE

Theodore Roosevelt threw himself into frontier life with abandon—at times with reckless abandon. He wanted desperately to be an authentic cowboy.

He placed a trio of boat thieves under citizen's arrest and marched them at gunpoint to the sheriff in Dickinson. He punched out a drunken gunslinger in a saloon. He made long solo hunting trips through the wilderness. He rode night guard during the long regional roundups. He branded calves.

And he helped stop stampedes.

The most dramatic stampede began at a wide bottom on the west bank of the Little Missouri River near the base of Chimney Butte, a few miles south of Medora. As evening approached a massive thunderstorm began to move in from the west. The cattle were restless and uneasy.

Lincoln Lang, one of the night herders, feared trouble and sent a call around the camp of "all hands out." The always-enthusiastic Roosevelt jumped on a horse. Just then a bolt of lightning struck near the enormous herd of cattle.

The cattle stampeded.

To stop the stampede and prevent cattle from scattering in every direction, cowboys had to race ahead of the terrified cattle and turn the herd back onto itself. This is easier said than done, even in broad daylight. As Roosevelt later described it, it was a pitch black night except when lightning provided a nanosecond's strobe illumination of the terrain. Roosevelt could make out the dark forms of cattle, and he could hear horns clash when they collided and the thunder of hooves on the ground.

Roosevelt galloped forward in the dark to try to reach leaders of the stampede and turn them. He knew that if he fell off his horse, he might be trampled to death. He was terrified and exhilarated. This was precisely the reason he had invested in frontier ranches—to get access to the raw and authentic experiences of the American West.

Suddenly Roosevelt heard splashing. Before he could process this information, his horse plunged over the bank of the Little Missouri River and into the shallow stream. His horse tripped and lurched but somehow stayed on his feet, churned knee deep through the water, and struggled up the other bank. Roosevelt had narrowly escaped death in the river.

> *It was really one of the worst mix-ups I ever saw.*
>
> — LINCOLN LANG

Roosevelt's friend Frederic Remington produced this illustration of the stampede.

Now he was racing across the plains again on the east bank of the Little Missouri. He was aware for a moment that another rider was right beside him. Then he was gone. A few minutes later TR's horse tripped and did a complete somersault, throwing Roosevelt to the ground. He remounted and resumed the chase. The cowboys managed to stop the stampede three times that night, and three times it started up again.

Lincoln Lang later wrote, "I don't know how we ever got through. All we had was lightning flashes to go by. It was really one of the worst mix-ups I ever saw. That surely was a night."

When day broke, Roosevelt drove the last strays towards camp. On the way, he encountered a cowboy on foot. It was the man he had seen for an instant at the height of the storm. His horse had run into a tree in the dark and been instantly killed.

The ranchers of the western frontier believed that the law alone could not curtail rustling.

"I have not a particle of sympathy with the sentimentality—as I deem it, the mawkishness—which overflows with foolish pity for the criminal and cares not at all for the victim of the criminal. I am glad to see wrong-doers punished. The punishment is an absolute necessity from the standpoint of society; and I put the reformation of the criminal second to the welfare of society. But I do desire to see the man or woman who has paid the penalty and who wishes to reform given a helping hand—surely every one of us who knows his own heart must know that he too may stumble, and should be anxious to help his brother or sister who has stumbled. When the criminal has been punished, if he then shows a sincere desire to lead a decent and upright life, he should be given the chance, he should be helped and not hindered; and if he makes good, he should receive that respect from others which so often aids in creating self-respect—the most invaluable of all possessions."

*Autobiography*

# ROOSEVELT AND THE VIGILANTES

When Theodore Roosevelt lived in Dakota Territory (1883-87), the institutions of law and order had not really found their way to one of America's last frontiers.

Horse-rustling had reached epidemic proportions in the badlands region. A Lewistown, Montana, newspaper reported that several hundred horses had been stolen over the winter of 1883-84. The *Bad Lands Cow Boy* estimated that 200 horses had been stolen on the Dakota side of the border alone. *The Dickinson Press* declared that while it was not generally in favor of lynch law, given the epidemic of thievery, "we think if their bodies were made to stretch a few yards of hemp it would have a salutary effect."

*❝...we think if their bodies were made to stretch a few yards of hemp it would have a salutary effect. ❞*

— THE DICKINSON PRESS

Although Roosevelt and the Marquis de Mores (the French aristocrat who founded Medora) were never close friends, they shared a sense of noblesse oblige, and they both had a highly advanced sense of honor. They were also both adventure-junkies and natural romantics. It was inevitable, therefore, that they would want to join cattleman Granville Stuart's band of vigilantes who were taking the law into their own hands to clear horse thieves out of the territory. De Mores joined to protect his property, Roosevelt because there was no ritual or aspect of frontier life that he did not want to immerse himself in.

A group of grim vigilantes prepares to enforce the rough justice of the frontier.

Granville Stuart (1834–1918) was a man almost as colorful as Theodore Roosevelt. He was a Montana cattle baron, a Gold Rush miner, and leader of vigilantes. He was also the U.S. ambassador to Paraguay and Uruguay, and the author of a remarkable autobiography, *Forty Years on the Frontier.* Although he married a Shoshone woman and mastered her language, Stuart disowned their 11 children at the time of his second marriage to a white woman.

De Mores and Roosevelt rode a train to Glendive, Montana, in June 1884, to sign up. Granville Stuart refused to let them join the mounted group of "stranglers." He told them they were both too "socially prominent" for such grim and anonymous business. Stuart, a man of extraordinary intelligence, undoubtedly knew that Roosevelt was not merely prominent, but unlikely to be able to keep his mouth shut about frontier adventures of such drama and excitement.

Although Roosevelt was a severe opponent of the lynching of African Americans, he had a kind of romantic's sympathy for frontier vigilantism. "Generally," he wrote, "the vigilantes, by a series of summary executions, do really good work; but I have rarely known them fail, among the men whom they killed for good reason, to also kill one or two either by mistake or to gratify private malice."

Stuart's vigilantes rooted out and hanged a number of horse thieves in the summer of 1884. Roosevelt later wrote that the stranglers "shot or hung nearly sixty" men altogether.

Roosevelt wisely never mentioned his flirtation with vigilantism in his correspondence or in the tens of thousands of words he wrote about his experiences in Dakota Territory. It is hard to imagine that he could have become president of the United States had he participated in this kind of extra-constitutional violence.

After his swim among the ice floes, Roosevelt bought new socks at Joe Ferris's store.

"When the days have dwindled to their shortest, and the nights seem never-ending, then all the great northern plains are changed into an abode of iron desolation. Sometimes furious gales blow down from the north, driving before them the clouds of blinding snow-dust, wrapping the mantle of death round every unsheltered being that faces their unshackled anger. They roar in a thunderous bass as they sweep across the prairie or whirl through the naked canyons; they shiver the great brittle cottonwoods, and beneath their rough touch the icy limbs of the pines that cluster in the gorges sing like the chords of an Aeolian harp. Again, the coldest midwinter weather, not a breath of wind may stir; and then the still, merciless, terrible cold that broods over the earth like the shadow of silent death seems even more dreadful in its gloomy rigor than is the lawless madness of the storms."

*Hunting Trips of a Ranchman*

# The Ice Capades of Theodore Roosevelt

**W**hen Theodore Roosevelt lived in the Dakota badlands, the Northern Pacific railroad bridge in Medora was the only bridge over the Little Missouri River.

The Little Missouri River runs high for a few weeks per year, then settles into a lovely sluggishness. Between May and November, the river is likely to be no more than a foot deep. When Roosevelt brought his wife Edith and his sisters to the badlands in 1890, the touring party forded the Little Missouri 23 times between Medora and his Elkhorn Ranch 35 miles north of here. It was that shallow.

It was (and is) common to cross the river at gravelly shallows, hoping that one's vehicle (horse, carriage, or car) would not get bogged down in mud and occasional quicksand in the riverbed. Roosevelt regarded all of this with strenuous nonchalance. The only time he had trouble crossing the Little Missouri River occurred in the spring of 1885, when the winter ice was breaking up. Most folks were crossing the river that spring on the NP railroad bridge, using a narrow footpath between tracks on the trestle. Not Roosevelt. That would be too easy.

**T**he Marquis de Mores had built a dam on the river to harvest ice of a certain thickness for his refrigerating plant. (The French aristocrat had built a slaughterhouse in Medora. He was sending dressed beef

Roosevelt sometimes pursued the strenuous life recklessly.

> **" Where does the dam start? "**
> —Theodore Roosevelt

to eastern markets with the help of the newly-invented refrigerator cars). Roosevelt had heard that courageous riders sometimes crossed the river by tiptoeing their horses along the narrow crest of de Mores' earthen dam. The problem on this April 1885 morning was that the river was flowing high over the top of the dam. The murkiness of the ice-clogged water made it impossible to see the narrow path.

Undaunted, Roosevelt approached the river. A friend named Fisher happened to be at the river's edge.

"Where does the dam start?" Roosevelt asked.

"You surely won't try to cross on the dam, when you can go and cross on the trestle the way the others do?" Fisher replied.

"If Manitou gets his feet on that dam, he'll keep them there and we can make it finely."

**S**o Roosevelt and his favorite horse began to pick their way across the swollen river. It looked as if he was going to make the transit successfully. People

had gathered on both sides of the river to watch the New York dude in action.

Suddenly, observers saw Roosevelt and Manitou simply disappear, swallowed up by the river. In a few seconds Roosevelt popped up, flung himself from his horse, and with one hand on the saddle horn swam to shore, pushing ice floes out of Manitou's path. Fisher and other witnesses were amazed that Roosevelt hadn't drowned in the cold, swift, clogged stream.

Finally, the two bedraggled creatures crawled up the east bank of the Little Missouri, soaked and chilled, but no worse for wear. Roosevelt was still wearing his famous spectacles. He waved to the crowd and laughed heartily, then mounted Manitou and rode to Joe Ferris' store, where he promptly bought a pair of dry socks.

Ferris was dumbfounded. "Landsake, man! Weren't you afraid?"

**"I** was riding Manitou," Roosevelt replied, and proceeded on his journey.

De Mores abandoned his Medora-to-Deadwood Stage Line as quickly as he envisioned it.

It is true of the Nation, as of the individual, that the greatest doer must also be a great dreamer. Of course, if the dream is not followed by action, then it is a bubble; it has merely served to divert the man from doing something. But great action, action that is really great, can not take place if the man has it not in his brain to think great thoughts, to dream great dreams.

Address at Clark University
June 21, 1905

# THE MARQUIS DE MORES: FRENCH ARISTOCRAT

One of the most colorful and controversial characters of the early Dakota badlands was the French nobleman the Marquis de Mores. Theodore Roosevelt and the Marquis had much in common. They were both aristocrats, one French, the other an American of Dutch descent, seeking adventures in the badlands. They were almost identical in age. They came to the badlands about the same time (1883) and left about the same time (1887). They both regarded the badlands as a place to make money, to hunt, and commune with the essence of the American West.

There were essential differences, too. Though Roosevelt was born into wealth and privilege in New York, he came to the badlands to experience one of the last remnants of the raw American frontier. He ached to become a genuine American cowboy and did what he could to squeeze every wholesome experience out of his sojourn, no matter how exhausting, dirty, or humble the work. He spent weeks participating in cattle roundups and helped to stop stampedes. He ate the common grub of the frontier around the fire with cowboys who would never be admitted to his social clubs in New York.

The Marquis de Mores regarded himself as a feudal lord in the badlands. He built a ridgeline house on a bluff overlooking the Little Missouri River. It was a rudimentary house for a man who believed he was descended from royalty and had a distant claim to the French crown, but local folks regarded it as a mansion or, as they put it, the Chateau de Mores.

Instead of mingling with local folks, the Marquis held himself aloof. At a time when the badlands were still open range, he purchased all the land he wanted, drove squatters away, and—to make matters much worse—fenced his properties. To protect his fences and his status as seigneur of the territory, he killed a man in a cold-blooded ambush not long before Roosevelt first arrived.

> Roosevelt ached to become a genuine American cowboy.

When folks of the village of Little Missouri failed to hearken to De Mores' haughty commands, he simply purchased land on the other side of the river and founded his own town, which he named Medora in honor of his wife.

The dashing Marquis de Mores in his prime.

De Mores was born on June 14, 1858, in Paris. In 1879 he graduated from St. Cyr, the premier military academy in France, then attended the leading cavalry school in France. He posted to Algiers to help put down an uprising and fought his first duel. In 1882 in Paris, he married Medora von Hoffman, daughter of a wealthy New York banker. He came to the badlands to hunt, and he stayed to make a fortune. The Marquis was a quixotic dreamer. He wanted to slaughter cattle in the badlands, then ship the dressed beef to market in newly-invented refrigerator cars.

De Mores' entrepreneurial dreams eventually collapsed. The beef industry did what it could to prevent his success. He invested in too many enterprises too quickly, and made enemies wherever he went.

By 1887 he was gone, though the romantic adventures of his life were far from over. Unlike Roosevelt, he never returned.

De Mores was assassinated by Tuareg tribesmen in Algeria on June 9, 1896. He was 37 years old.

The Marquis de Mores, armed and always on hand.

"Death is always and under all circumstances a tragedy, for if it is not, then it means that life itself has become one. But it is well to live bravely and joyously, and to face the inevitable end without flinching, when we go to join the men and the tribes of immemorial eld. Death is the one thing certain for the nation as for the man, though from the loins of the one as from the loins of the other descendants may spring to carry on through the ages the work done by the dead."

To Cecil Spring Rice
March 12, 1900

# The "Duel" with the Marquis de Mores

Theodore Roosevelt and French nobleman the Marquis de Mores were the two most socially prominent men in the Dakota badlands between 1883 and 1887. They circled each other with wary friendliness and eventually fell into a serious dispute.

De Mores had imperiously grazed his cattle on Roosevelt's Maltese Cross acreage in 1884. He also challenged Roosevelt's right to establish his second ranch, the Elkhorn, where he did; Roosevelt shrugged off the protest. On another occasion, de Mores contracted to buy some of Roosevelt's cattle at a certain price. When TR drove the cattle to the Marquis' slaughterhouse in Medora, the French land baron unilaterally reduced the payment. Roosevelt turned his herd around and determined to have no further financial dealings with de Mores.

> " I am not your enemy; if I were you would know it, for I would be an open one... "
>
> — Theodore Roosevelt

The decisive break came in September 1885 when de Mores was on trial for murder in Mandan, Dakota Territory. Although murder charges against him had been dismissed twice before, in 1885 the Marquis was formally indicted by a grand jury for the murder of Riley Luffsey. The Marquis believed Roosevelt's friend Joe Ferris was rounding up witnesses against him with Roosevelt's backing. While awaiting trial, he wrote Roosevelt a remarkable letter on September 3, 1885.

My principle is to take the bull by the horns. Joe Ferris is very active against me and has been instrumental in getting me indicted by furnishing money to witnesses and hunting them up. The papers also publish very stupid accounts of our quarrelling—I sent you the paper to N.Y. Is this done by your orders? I thought you my friend. If you are my enemy I want to know it. I am always on hand as you know, and between gentlemen it is easy to settle matters of that sort directly.

Yours very truly,
Mores

Roosevelt regarded the letter as the threat of a duel. He was not eager to fight a man who was known to have killed at least one European opponent in a duel. But as a man who never shrank from challenges, Roosevelt could not afford to back down.

Knowing that de Mores exercised his fencing hand by holding a nine-pound cane horizontal to the ground, and that the Frenchman's eyesight was dramatically better

The Marquis de Mores was a serious duelist; Roosevelt, a man who never backed down.

than his own, Roosevelt shrewdly determined that if a duel came, the weapons should be rifles at twelve paces.

Then he replied to de Mores' letter:

Most emphatically I am not your enemy; if I were you would know it, for I would be an open one, and would not have asked you to my house nor gone to yours. As your final words, however, seem to imply a threat it is due to myself to say that the statement is not made through any fear of possible consequences to me; I too, as you know, am always at hand, and ever ready to hold myself accountable in any way for anything I have said or done.

Yours very truly,
Theodore Roosevelt

Nothing more came of the incident.

It seems clear that de Mores was not threatening a duel, though he was warning Roosevelt that he would not tolerate meddling in his legal affairs.

A.T. Packard was one of the first to predict that Roosevelt would be president of the United States.

"I think that if there is one thing we ought to be careful about it is in regard to interfering with the liberty of the press. We have all of us at times suffered from the liberty of the press, but we have to take the good and the bad. I think we certainly ought to hesitate very seriously before passing any law that will interfere with the broadest public utterance. I think it is a great deal better to err a little bit on the side of having too much discussion and having too virulent language used by the press, rather than to err on the side of having them not say what they ought to say, especially with reference to public men and measures."

Remarks in the New York Assembly
March 27, 1883

# MEDORA JOURNALIST A.T. PACKARD

Theodore Roosevelt first met Arthur Packard in September 1883 in Bismarck. Packard was then the editor of the *Bismarck Tribune*.

Packard was a young, thoughtful, and sometimes sardonic graduate of the University of Michigan who had come to Dakota Territory to experience one of the last wild frontiers of America. Less than a year out of college, he started at the *Bismarck Tribune*, then transferred to the *Mandan Pioneer*, and wound up creating Medora's *Bad Lands Cow Boy*, one of the most important historical records of Roosevelt's time in Dakota Territory.

Packard established *Bad Lands Cow Boy* in February 1884, "not for fun," as he put it in the first issue, "but for $2 per year." Historian Hermann Hagedorn writes that although the lawlessness of Medora did not abate, Packard's newspaper brought "a somewhat shy and wraithlike civilization" to the territory.

"Every printed word," Packard remembered, "bore my brand... There was no libel law; no law of any kind except six shooter rights. And I was the only man who never carried a six-shooter."

When Packard first arrived, he sat in a saloon taking notes about a classical cowboy standing against the wall. Eventually the cowboy noticed Packard staring at him, then scribbling notes. Packard was merely writing a descriptive letter to his family back in Indiana. He intended to take the letter to the telegraph office. When he opened the door, an icy blast of air caused him to rethink the errand. He'd mail the letter tomorrow.

The next afternoon, Packard was riding towards the Maltese Cross Ranch, seven miles south of Medora, when the same cowboy suddenly joined his ride. "So you're a newspaper feller. That's damn funny. You see, Frank Moore he said you was a deputy sheriff on the

BAD LANDS COW BOY,

BY A. T. PACKARD.

THE COW BOY is not published for fun, but for $2 per year.

Advertising Rates made known on application.

Standing Advertisements payable quarterly.

Transient Advertisements and all Job work, money in sight.

Address all communications to

THE BAD LANDS COW BOY,
MEDORA, DAKOTA.

The *Bad Lands Cow Boy* is the best record we have of Roosevelt's time in Dakota Territory.

lookout for a horse thief. Where was you going last night when you started to go out?"

> ‟ I was the only man who never carried a six-shooter. ”
>
> —ARTHUR T. PACKARD

"To the telegraph office," Packard said.

"Well, if you'd gone, I'd have killed you."

Roosevelt liked to spend time with Packard because he was literate, politically astute, and more enlightened than the usual saloon crawler of the badlands.

Packard convinced Roosevelt not to pack a pistol. "The majority of gun-toters," he explained, "could draw and shoot one or more times before I could draw." To prove his point, Packard had local gunman William

Roberts demonstrate his ability to shoot two airborne tomato cans simultaneously.

Packard played an important role in organizing Billings County. He was elected police commissioner, though he had no budget, no equipment, and no cops.

Packard accompanied Roosevelt to the Independence Day celebration in Dickinson, Dakota Territory, on July 4, 1886. They traveled the 35 miles by freight train. After listening to TR's first great national speech in Dickinson, Packard predicted that Roosevelt would one day become president of the United States.

"If your prophecy comes true, I will do my best to make a good one." TR replied.

Packard suspended publication of *Bad Lands Cow Boy* on December 23, 1886, and moved to Montana.

An unidentified badlands cowboy plunges to the dust.

"You are all off about my horsemanship; as you would say if you saw me now. Almost all of our horses on the ranch being young, I had to include in my string three that were but partially broken; and I have had some fine circuses with them. One of them had never been saddled but once before, and he proved vicious, and besides bucking, kept falling over backwards with me; finally he caught me, giving me an awful slam, from which my left arm has by no means recovered. Another bucked me off going down hill; but I think I have cured him, for I put him through a desperate course of sprouts when I got on him again. The third I nearly lost in swimming him across a swollen creek, where the flood had carried down a good deal of drift timber."

To Henry Cabot Lodge
June 5, 1885

# ROOSEVELT AND BUCKING HORSES

Theodore Roosevelt had never saddled his own horse until he came to the Dakota badlands. He had ridden a fair amount on Long Island, but in that aristocratic world, grooms prepared the horses for gentlemen riders. In Dakota Territory, Roosevelt spent many hours in the saddle. His favorite horse was Manitou, "stoutly built and strong... perfectly sure-footed and as fast as any horse on the river. Though both willing and spirited, he is very gentle..."

During his four-year sojourn (1883-87) in the badlands, Roosevelt rode plenty of wild horses, sometimes because he had no choice, sometimes because local pranksters wanted to watch the greenhorn get bucked off. Roosevelt was invariably a good sport.

Roosevelt was not exactly fearless, but he was courageous. In his *Autobiography* (1913), Roosevelt wrote, "There were all kinds of things I was afraid of at first, ranging from grizzly bears to 'mean' horses and gun-fighters; but by acting as if I was not afraid I gradually ceased to be afraid."

Fellow cowboy Lincoln Lang described an occasion when Roosevelt rode "a bad horse" during the 1885 spring roundup. "He didn't know much about that kind of riding, but meant to stay at all costs." The horse had been blindfolded. Roosevelt gripped the saddle horn with his right hand and the back of the saddle with his left. Lang said there was "ever a certain stigma attaching to holding on in this

Roosevelt (not pictured here) was never afraid to mount a troublesome horse.

way, but there was a still worse stigma attached to getting thrown, and Roosevelt was wisely choosing the lesser evil."

The horse arched its back so completely that its head was almost on the ground and its front and hind feet were drawn nearly together. "Forward, upward, sidewise, the star performer projected himself into the

> **" ... by acting as if I was not afraid I gradually ceased to be afraid. "**
>
> — THEODORE ROOSEVELT

air, landing stiff legged and rebounding forcefully. Roosevelt managed to stay on the horse. Like a burr, he stuck, until a couple boys induced the animal to break and run for it."

Eventually Roosevelt returned, looking none the worse for wear.

Lang acknowledged that Roosevelt took a beating on that horse. Still, Roosevelt never complained about his bruises, never regarded himself as special for having ridden a difficult horse. He regarded it as nothing more or less than the daily life of the working cowboy.

On another occasion, Roosevelt added what historian Hermann Hagedorn called "a great man-killing bronco, with a treacherous streak" to his roundup string against the protests of his own men. When Roosevelt mounted the horse, it reared and fell over backward on the future president. Roosevelt discovered that the point of his shoulder was broken. Since the nearest doctor was at least 40 miles away, he simply lived with the pain and let the shoulder slowly heal itself.

"Some of those Eastern punkin-lilies now," said TR's friend Dutch Wannigan, "those goody-goody fellows, if they'd ever get throwed off you'd never hear the last of it. He didn't care a bit. By gollies, if he got throwed off, he'd get right on again."

Roosevelt's photograph of the Elkhorn Ranch from the opposite side of the Little Missouri River.

"The ranch house stood on the brink of a low bluff overlooking the broad, shallow bed of the Little Missouri, through which at most seasons there ran only a trickle of water, while in times of freshet it was filled brimful with the boiling, foaming, muddy torrent. There was no neighbor for ten or fifteen miles on either side of me. The river twisted down in long curves between narrow bottoms bordered by sheer cliff walls, for the Bad Lands, a chaos of peaks, plateaus, and ridges, rose abruptly from the edges of the level, tree-clad, or grassy, alluvial meadows. In front of the ranch-house veranda was a row of cottonwood trees with gray-green leaves which quivered all day long if there was a breath of air."

*Autobiography*

# ROOSEVELT AND THE ELKHORN RANCH

Theodore Roosevelt made his first trip to the Dakota badlands in September 1883. Captivated by the place, he impulsively invested in a ranch south of Medora. On that journey, he was a young man whose life was completely on track. When he returned to the badlands in June 1884, Roosevelt was a man in spiritual disarray. He was still in acute grief over the death of his first wife Alice. She had died on Valentine's Day 1884, just two days after giving birth to their first child, Alice.

Theodore Roosevelt took this photograph of the Elkhorn Ranch.

In June 1884, the future president discovered that his Maltese Cross Ranch was on a well-traveled trail. He wanted to grieve in solitude. He also needed a place where he could work on writing projects.

On one of his solo rides down the Little Missouri River, Roosevelt ran into Howard Eaton. Roosevelt said he was looking for a second ranch. Eaton told him of an ideal site about five miles from his own ranch on Big Beaver Creek. Roosevelt made an inspection on horseback. The site was remote and located in one of the most beautiful places in the badlands. At the edge of the river he found the mingled antlers of two elk who had gotten locked together in a mortal fight. He determined on the spot that this would be his home ranch and that he would call it the Elkhorn.

Roosevelt bought rights to the site from the existing squatter for $400.

He imported two acquaintances from Maine to manage the Elkhorn Ranch. One was William Sewall, his guide during the years he sought to toughen up body and spirit in Maine. The other was Sewall's nephew, Wilmot Dow.

With a modest amount of help from Roosevelt, Sewall and Dow cut down trees and built a 60-by-30 foot cabin at the Elkhorn site, 35 miles north of Medora. The low building, seven feet high, had eight rooms and a porch fronting on the Little Missouri River. The ranch hands also constructed a barn consisting of two stables, a cattle shed, a chicken house, and a blacksmith shop.

> " This is the last year
> I shall keep the
> ranch house open. "
>
> — THEODORE ROOSEVELT

Dow and Sewall were less optimistic than Roosevelt about prospects for economic success in the Little Missouri River Valley. They stayed until winter 1886, when they returned to Maine.

Roosevelt found solitude at the Elkhorn Ranch. He wrote parts of several books there, read deeply, and sat for long hours in his rocking chair on the piazza observing the river.

Roosevelt's ranches survived the disastrous blizzards of 1886-87, but as his political career in the East revived, his grief began to recede. He fell in love with and married his childhood sweetheart Edith Carow. TR began to pull away from Dakota Territory. After a late summer visit in 1890, he more or less abandoned the Elkhorn Ranch. On October 20, 1890, he wrote to Sewall, "This is the last year I shall keep the ranch house open; I have just parted with Merrifield. Sylvane will take care of the cattle now."

Roosevelt's last known visit to the Elkhorn was in 1892. Today the site is owned and managed by the National Park Service. At 218 acres, it is the smallest of the three units of Theodore Roosevelt National Park.

Roosevelt advised others to avoid fights if they could, but–once in–to make sure the other guy couldn't get up!

"As I rose, I struck quick and hard with my right just to one side of the point of his jaw, hitting with my left as I straightened out, and then again with my right. He fired the guns, but I do not know whether this was merely a convulsive action of his hands or whether he was trying to shoot at me. When he went down he struck the corner of the bar with his head. It was not a case in which one could afford to take chances, and if he had moved I was about to drop on his ribs with my knees; but he was senseless. I took away his guns, and the other people in the room, who were now loud in their denunciation of him, hustled him out and put him in a shed. I got dinner as soon as possible, sitting in a corner of the dining room away from the windows, and then went upstairs to be where it was dark so that there would be no chance of any one shooting at me from the outside."

*Autobiography*

# ROOSEVELT AND THE DRUNKEN GUNSLINGER

Out searching for stray horses on the open range and needing a place to stay, Theodore Roosevelt rode into Mingusville (now Wibaux), Montana, sometime during his badlands sojourn, probably in the early summer of 1885.

He took a room at Nolan's Hotel. Hungry for a beefsteak, he was advised that his only option was the saloon in the hotel. Now Roosevelt was very nearly a teetotaler, a sarsaparilla man, and he was not fond of bars and saloons. But he was hungry as a wolf, so he ventured through the doors of the saloon like a character in a dime novel.

Inside the dimly lit saloon, all was chaos. A drunken gunslinger, with a pistol in either hand, was shooting up the bar and menacing the terrified patrons. Roosevelt somehow thought he could slip into a back table without attracting attention. The desperado noticed him immediately and loudly announced, "Four Eyes is going to treat."

Roosevelt later said he did not regard the ruffian as "a *bad man* of the really dangerous type," but that he was certainly "an objectionable creature." The future president laughed in a good-natured way and "got behind the stove and sat down, thinking to escape notice."

No chance of that. The gunman soon appeared at TR's table "leaning over me, a gun in each hand, using very foul language."

Roosevelt realized that he had happened upon one of the defining moments of his life.

The future president had studied boxing at Harvard, where he had proved to be a plucky if not very dominant pugilist. He noticed that the villain, in his inebriation, had placed his booted feet rather too close together; his center of gravity, therefore, was by no

Wibaux during the Roosevelt era.

means adequate. The next time the gunman insisted that Roosevelt buy a round for everyone, TR replied, "Well, if I've got to, I've got to."

Our hero Roosevelt tells it best. "As I rose, I struck quick and hard with my right just to one side of the point of his jaw, hitting with my left as I straightened out, and then again with my right."

Theodore Roosevelt, man of law, seeker of adventure.

As the ruffian fell, he hit his head on the bar and was knocked out cold. Roosevelt later reported in ecstasy that, as the ruffian fell, both pistols were discharged. TR was twice thrilled: to know that he had not been shot, but also to know that he *might* have been killed!

Roosevelt disarmed the gunman, who was hustled out by the suddenly brave saloon patrons and thrown into a shed. When he came to, "he went down to the station and left on a freight [train]."

Roosevelt—frontier hero, exemplar of law and order—sat down and finished his beefsteak.

Life in the American West doesn't get any better than this.

> *As I rose, I struck quick and hard with my right...*
>
> — THEODORE ROOSEVELT

Roosevelt riding to Glenwood Springs, Colorado, after a bear hunt, 1905.

"The grizzly is now chiefly a beast of the high hills and heavy timber;
but this is merely because he has learned that he must rely on
cover to guard him from man, and has forsaken the open ground
accordingly. In old days, and in one or two very out-of-the-way places
almost to the present time, he wandered at will over the plains. It is only the
wariness born of fear which nowadays causes him to cling to the thick brush
of the large river-bottoms throughout the plains country. When there were
no rifle-bearing hunters in the land, to harass him and make him afraid, he
roved hither and thither at will, in burly self-confidence."

*The Wilderness Hunter*

# ROOSEVELT AND THE GRIZZLY BEAR

In the course of his hectic life, Theodore Roosevelt sought to kill one of everything—deer, birds, mountain sheep, elk, rhinoceros, elephants, lions, cougars, bears, jaguars, hippopotami... And on and on. It would be impossible to tally the number of animals he killed in his six decades of hunting, but the number would be staggering.

And yet Roosevelt was one of the great conservationists of American history. It's a paradox.

He bagged his first grizzly bear in the Big Horn Mountains of Wyoming in autumn of 1884. Roosevelt was still grieving the death of his first wife Alice at the time of the 600-mile, two-month journey. He left his Maltese Cross Ranch on August 18, 1884, with his ranch hand William Merrifield and a teamster named Norman Lebo, whom TR described as a "chatty, tough old plainsman, full of expedients and ready with both wit and hands." Merrifield was a hard-working ranch hand who had an outsized ego, an at-times condescending attitude towards Roosevelt, particularly on hunting matters, and a belief that women found him irresistible.

"We had no directions as to where the Big Horn Mountains were," Merrifield later recalled, "except that they lay to the southwest." They traveled up (south on) the Little Missouri River to Lake Station (today's Baker, Montana), then up the Powder River until it was necessary to veer off towards the Big Horns. They hunted all the way and arrived at Buffalo, Wyoming, on September 1.

The hunting party spent two weeks in the pristine Big Horn Mountains.

Roosevelt got his grizzly on September 13. Merrifield saw the bear first, but he let Roosevelt have the glory. "Merrifield sank suddenly on one knee," Roosevelt wrote, "turning half round, his face fairly aflame with excitement; and as I strode past him, with my rifle at the ready, there, not ten steps off, was the great bear, slowly rising from his bed among the young spruces."

> *"The bullet hole in his skull was exactly between his eyes as if I measured the distance with a carpenter's rule."*
> — THEODORE ROOSEVELT

President Roosevelt takes aim at a bear.

"His head was slightly down, and when I saw the top of the white bead fairly between his small, glittering, evil eyes, I pulled the trigger. Half rising up, the huge beast fell over on his side in the death throes, the ball having gone through his brain.

As I pulled the trigger I jumped aside out of the smoke, to be ready if he charged; but it was needless, for the great brute was struggling in the death agony..."

When Roosevelt was able to inspect the dead grizzly bear he discovered, with infinite delight, that "the bullet hole in his skull was as exactly between his eyes as if I had measured the distance with a carpenter's rule."

Merrifield later provided a rather amusing account of the great event. "Roosevelt got pretty excited," he recalled. "He was going to keep on shooting. I said, 'You've killed him. You hit him right between the eyes.'... Roosevelt grabbed me and wouldn't let me go. He said, 'My good man, I will always do as you say.'"

It was Theodore Roosevelt's first grizzly bear, but it would not be his last.

Roosevelt staged this photo of his arrest of the boat thieves to illustrate the articles he wrote about his adventure as deputy sheriff.

"I have not a particle of sympathy with the sentimentality—as I deem it, the mawkishness—which overflows with foolish pity for the criminal and cares not at all for the victim of the criminal. I am glad to see wrong-doers punished. The punishment is an absolute necessity from the standpoint of society; and I put the reformation of the criminal second to the welfare of society. But I do desire to see the man or woman who has paid the penalty and who wishes to reform given a helping hand—surely every one of us who knows his own heart must know that he too may stumble, and should be anxious to help his brother or sister who has stumbled. When the criminal has been punished, if he then shows a sincere desire to lead a decent and upright life, he should be given the chance, he should be helped and not hindered; and if he makes good, he should receive that respect from others which so often aids in creating self-respect—the most invaluable of all possessions."

*Autobiography*

# ROOSEVELT AND THE BOAT THIEVES

Theodore Roosevelt kept one of the few boats on the Little Missouri River at his Elkhorn Ranch, 35 miles north of Medora. In the spring of 1886, Roosevelt's ranch manager Bill Sewall noticed that the boat was missing. The rope securing it to the river bank had been cut.

Roosevelt immediately concluded that Red Headed Mike Finnegan, a horse thief, had stolen the boat. TR's ranch hands, Bill Sewall and Wilmot Dow, determined that pursuing the thieves by horse would be impossible, given the sodden nature of the countryside.

They were not reckoning on their boss' devotion to law and order or his lively sense of adventure. Roosevelt ordered his men to build a makeshift boat. Meanwhile, a snowstorm swept across the Dakota badlands. Huge blocks of ice piled up along the river.

When the boat was ready, on March 30, 1886, the men packed two weeks of provisions and set out in pursuit of the boat thieves. "It was a strange, wild, desolate country ... that we passed through as we drifted with the current," Sewall later recalled.

On the third day out, Roosevelt's posse caught up with one thief at a campsite. They arrested him and learned that his two companions were off hunting. When Finnegan and his other partner, a man named Bernstead, returned, Roosevelt jumped forward and ordered them to drop their guns. Bernstead complied, but Finnegan, TR later reported, "hesitated for a second, his eyes fairly wolfish. Then, as I walked up within a few paces, covering the centre of his chest so as to avoid overshooting,... with an oath let his rifle drop and held his hands up beside his head."

Roosevelt's ranch hands prepare to pursue the boat thieves. Photo by Theodore Roosevelt.

Roosevelt had his boat thieves. Now he had to get them to an officer of the law. Roosevelt didn't dare tie them up at night for fear that they would suffer frostbite, so he made them relinquish their boots and socks, and the three-man posse mounted a 24-hour guard. For several days the six men floated down the river, but ice jams prevented them from progressing more than a few miles per day. Their food supply was running out.

Faced with the necessity of letting the thieves go or finding a different travel method, Roosevelt left Sewall and Dow behind and began to march the thieves overland to Dickinson (a distance of more than 40 miles). At a Killdeer Mountain ranch, Roosevelt managed to obtain additional supplies, a horse and wagon, and a ranch hand to drive it.

Alone with three men who were not eager to face justice, Roosevelt walked ankle deep in gumbo behind the wagon by day and stayed awake all night to make sure the desperadoes did not abscond—or worse. The forced march took nearly three days.

On April 11, Roosevelt reached Dickinson, turned the men over to the sheriff, and received a $50 reward. After being outside for almost two weeks, Roosevelt's feet were bruised, swollen, and infected. He was also, of course, exhausted.

> "He was all teeth and eyes, but even so he seemed a man unusually wide awake."
>
> — DR. VICTOR HUGO STICKNEY

On the street in Dickinson, Roosevelt encountered Dr. Victor Hugo Stickney, the only physician within 100 miles. Dr. Stickney attended to TR's feet, and they became fast friends. Stickney wrote, "He was all teeth and eyes, but even so he seemed a man unusually wide awake. You could see he was thrilled by the adventures he had been through."

Dickinson, N. D. 1883

Dickinson, North Dakota, the year Roosevelt first arrived in the badlands.

"We have fallen heirs to the most glorious heritage a people ever received, and each one must do his part if we wish to show that the nation is worthy of its good fortune. Here we are not ruled over by others as is the case in Europe; we rule ourselves. All American citizens, whether born here or elsewhere, whether of one creed or another, stand on the same footing. We welcome every honest immigrant, no matter from what country he comes, provided only that he leaves behind him his former nationality and remain neither Celt nor Saxon, neither Frenchman nor German, but become an American desirous of fulfilling in good faith the duties of American citizenship."

TR's Fourth of July Speech
Dickinson, Dakota Territory, 1886

"I think very little of mere oratory. I feel an impatient contempt for the man of words if he is merely a man of words. The great speech must be the speech of a man with a great soul, who has a thought worth putting into words, and whose acts bear out the words he utters; and the occasion must demand the speech."

To Henry Cabot Lodge
July 19, 1908

# ROOSEVELT'S FIRST GREAT NATIONAL SPEECH

In the course of his Dakota adventures, Theodore Roosevelt became friends with Dr. Victor Hugo Stickney of Dickinson, then a rude frontier town of approximately 500 residents. Stickney invited the 27-year-old Roosevelt to give the Fourth of July address at Dickinson's first-ever celebration of the birth of the United States.

Because no passenger train was available in Medora that morning, Roosevelt rode into Dickinson on a freight train. He was traveling with the young editor of the *Bad Lands Cow Boy*, Arthur Packard, and several others from the badlands.

Dickinson made up in enthusiasm what it lacked in sophistication. At 10 a.m. the parade began, featuring the Silver Cornet Band, followed by "lady equestriennes," a cluster of soldiers and veterans, a horse-drawn wagon carrying young girls in white dresses representing all 38 states in the union, farm equipment, and then the "Invincibles," a strolling company of local folks in masks and grotesque costumes. A witness later said, "The trouble with the parade was that everyone in town was so enthusiastic they insisted on joining the procession, and there was no one to watch except two men who were too drunk to notice anything."

It turned out to be a day of high winds. The justice of the peace, a man actually named Western Starr, read the Declaration of Independence. Lunch was served. Then two illustrious speakers addressed the multitude: John Rea, who gave a patriotic speech full of platitudes, and Roosevelt, who decided to speak straight from the heart.

> *" I am, myself, at heart as much a Westerner as an Easterner. "*
>
> — THEODORE ROOSEVELT

Roosevelt made clear how much he had gained from his sojourn in the Dakota badlands, how much his life had been changed by his adventures on the frontier. "I am, myself, at heart as much a Westerner as an Easterner," he said. "I am proud, indeed, to be considered one of yourselves."

Though witnesses said his voice registered somewhere "between a squeak and a shriek," Roosevelt spoke from the depths of his heroic soul:

"Like all Americans, I like big things." No photo exists of TR's Dickinson speech. But he probably gestured just like this.

> *"*Like all Americans, I like big things; big prairies, big forests and mountains, big wheat fields, railroads—and herds of cattle, too—big factories, steamboats, and everything else. But we must keep steadily in mind that no people were ever yet benefited by riches if their prosperity corrupted their virtue.*"*

It was Roosevelt's first great national speech, the first in which the man of destiny and the advocate of the strenuous life could be heard in full measure.

On the way back to Medora, this time on a passenger train, Roosevelt went on at considerable length about America's destiny, its need for good government, the duties of each citizen, and the responsibilities of leadership. Packard, who was just 24, listened to TR all the way out to the badlands. Before they pulled in to the station, Packard predicted that Roosevelt would someday become the president of the United States.

"If your prophecy comes true," Roosevelt replied, "I will do my part to make a good one."

Roosevelt posed for a photograph with the folks of Medora in April 1903.

"Do you know what chapter in all my life… looking back over all of it… I would choose to remember, were the alternative forced upon me to recall [only] one portion of it, and to have erased from my memory all other experiences? I would take the memory of my life on the ranch with its experiences close to nature and among the men who lived nearest her."

To New Mexico Senator Albert Fall
1904

# ROOSEVELT'S FOOTPRINT IN NORTH DAKOTA

Theodore Roosevelt famously said he would never have been president of the United States had it not been for the time he spent in North Dakota. Because he was the greatest conservationist in American presidential history, and because he dearly loved this place, Roosevelt gave North Dakota special attention during the seven years of his presidential tenure.

In 1903, President Roosevelt used an executive order to create the first Federal Bird Sanctuary on Pelican Island in the Indian River in Florida. Over the next five years, he designated 50 more bird sanctuaries in 16 states, plus Puerto Rico. These bird sanctuaries are now called National Wildlife Refuges.

Roosevelt designated two Federal Bird Sanctuaries in North Dakota. The first was Stump Lake in Nelson County, designated on March 9, 1905. Stump Lake adjoins Devils Lake. Roosevelt designated his second North Dakota bird sanctuary at Chase Lake on August 28, 1908. Chase Lake National Wildlife Refuge in east central North Dakota is one of North America's prime pelican breeding grounds.

Today North Dakota has 63 National Wildlife Refuges, more than any other state. They cover 290,000 acres.

Roosevelt convinced Congress to designate five new National Parks on his watch, one located in North Dakota. The president proclaimed Sullys Hill National Park in 1904. The 1,674 acre site near Devils Lake features marshes, wooded hills, and small herds of bison, elk, white tailed deer, and a small colony of prairie dogs. The park is named for General Alfred Sully, who led the U.S. Army's retaliation against the Dakota Indians (the

The Elkhorn Ranch from the east bank of the Little Missouri. Roosevelt took this photograph.

Sioux) throughout Dakota Territory in the years following the Minnesota Uprising of 1862. On March 3, 1931, Congress dissolved Sullys Hill National Park and transferred jurisdiction of the lands to the U.S. Fish and Wildlife Service. Sullys Hill is one of just seven National Parks to have been disbanded.

Theodore Roosevelt played no role in the creation of Theodore Roosevelt National Park, which was not established until 1947, 28 years after his death. The park commemorates Roosevelt's life in the Dakota badlands and his extraordinary commitment to conservation of natural resources.

Although North Dakota is one of the most treeless regions in North America, Roosevelt did manage to designate one small National Forest in his beloved badlands. On November 24, 1908, he designated 13,940 acres near Amidon as the Dakota National Forest. On July 30, 1917, the Wilson administration abolished the forest, located approximately 40 miles south of Medora. No wonder Roosevelt disliked President Wilson!

In 1902 Roosevelt signed the Newlands Reclamation Act, a Congressional initiative to "make the desert bloom." The Newlands Act authorized the federal government to work with

> *It was still the Wild West in those days…It was a land of vast silent spaces, of lonely rivers, and of plains where the wild game stared at the passing horseman.*
>
> — THEODORE ROOSEVELT

western farmers to create dams and irrigation systems in arid regions. Roosevelt designated 24 federal reclamation projects in 14 states. The Lower Yellowstone Project was established on May 10, 1904, near the confluence of the Missouri and Yellowstone Rivers southwest of Williston, North Dakota. The project continues today.

In addition to all of this, Roosevelt's 1883-87 badlands sojourn gave North Dakota one of the most colorful chapters of its history. He was, arguably, the greatest man who ever lived amongst us. He left an indelible footprint on the mythology of North Dakota. Today's Medora is a living historical playground in which Theodore Roosevelt remains the central figure.

Roosevelt's companion P.B. Stewart, photographs a mountain lion, 1905.

"**B**oone's claim to distinction rests not so much on his wide wanderings in unknown lands, for in this respect he did little more than was done by a hundred other backwoods hunters of his generation, but on the fact that he was able to turn his daring woodcraft to the advantage of his fellows. As he himself said, he was an instrument 'ordained of God to settle the wilderness.' He inspired confidence in all who met him, so that the men of means and influence were willing to trust adventurous enterprises to his care; and his success as an explorer, his skill as a hunter, and his prowess as an Indian fighter, enabled him to bring these enterprises to a successful conclusion, and in some degree to control the wild spirits associated with him."

*The Winning of the West*

# ROOSEVELT AND THE BOONE AND CROCKETT CLUB

As soon as he finished his four-year sojourn in the American West (1883-1887), much of it spent in the Dakota badlands, Theodore Roosevelt joined with George Bird Grinnell to create the Boone and Crockett Club.

Roosevelt was thrilled to shoot buffalo, elk, grizzly bears, pronghorn antelope, bighorn sheep, and deer, but he realized—while he lived in the Dakota badlands—those species were in danger of becoming extinct because of homesteading and over-hunting. He wanted to conserve the great game species, partly because he found them surpassingly beautiful, and partly because he wanted to make sure future generations would have the same hunting opportunities he had so enjoyed.

George Bird Grinnell (1849-1938) was an anthropologist, a naturalist, and a historian. He had accompanied Lt. Col. George Custer on his 1874 reconnaissance of the Black Hills and declined to accompany Custer in 1876 to the Little Big Horn. From 1876-1911, Grinnell was the editor of America's leading outdoor magazine, *Field and Stream.* He also created the Audubon Society.

Roosevelt and Grinnell created the Boone and Crockett Club in December 1887. The dozen charter members met in January 1888 to approve the club's bylaws. The club would promote "manly sport with the rifle," "travel and exploration in the wild and unknown, or but partially known portions of the country," "work for the preservation of the large game of this country, and so far as possible further legislation for that purpose, and assist in enforcing the existing laws," promote the study of natural history, and "bring about among the members interchange of opinion and ideas on hunting, travel, and exploration."

It was an ambitious and far-reaching mission.

To be eligible to join, a hunter must have bagged three varieties of North American big game with a rifle. Members were sworn to maintain a strict code of honor—always to engage in "fair chase," never to lie about a kill, and always to maintain a focus on natural history as well as hunting.

The club was named after two of Theodore Roosevelt's heroes: Daniel Boone (1734-1820), who blazed the trail through the Cumberland Gap into the American interior in Kentucky, and Davy Crockett (1786-1836), representative from Tennessee in the U.S. House of Representatives, later killed at the Battle of the Alamo on March 6, 1836. Both were hunters, warriors, and icons of the American frontier.

A few of Roosevelt's trophies at Sagamore Hill.

The Boone and Crockett Club played a role in saving the buffalo and in saving Yellowstone National Park from commercial exploitation. The club's work on behalf of Yellowstone National Park inaugurated a new era in conservation history. Historian Douglas Brinkley has argued that "the Boone and Crockett Club—Roosevelt's brainchild—was the first wildlife organization group to lobby effectively on behalf of big game." Roosevelt remained president of the club until 1894.

Later in his career, Roosevelt realized that organizations like the Boone and Crockett Club could not alone save American wildlife. Private foundations would need to work with government to conserve what remained of the wild places and wild creatures of America. As president, Roosevelt extended the federal government into the cause of conservation in historically unprecedented ways.

> *We are prone to speak of the resources of this country as inexhaustible; this is not so.*
> — THEODORE ROOSEVELT,
> *Seventh Annual Message to Congress,*
> *December 3, 1907*

Roosevelt later regretted that he had not received a ghastly wound in Cuba.

"The men who made up the bulk of the regiment, and gave it its peculiar character... came from the four Territories which yet remained within the boundaries of the United States; that is, from the lands that have been most recently won over to white civilization, and in which the conditions of life are nearest those that obtained on the frontier when there still was a frontier. They were a splendid set of men, these southwesterners—tall and sinewy, with resolute, weather-beaten faces, and eyes that looked a man straight in the face without flinching. They included in their ranks men of every occupation; but the three types were those of the cowboy, the hunter, and the mining prospector—the man who wandered hither and thither, killing game for a living, and spending his life in the quest for metal wealth."

*The Rough Riders*

# THEODORE ROOSEVELT'S "CROWDED HOUR"

**S**ecretary of State John Hay called it a "splendid little war."

The minute the United States declared war on Spain on April 21, 1898, over the objections of just about everyone, Theodore Roosevelt resigned his position as assistant secretary of the U.S. Navy. For many years he had wanted to form a company of "harum-scarum roughriders" to ride heroically into war.

Now he had his chance.

**R**oosevelt gathered what he called a heterogeneous group of cowboys and Indians, Yale and Harvard high jumpers, tennis champions, football and polo players, a master of hounds, and a steeplechase rider. Among the westerners were a sheriff, a marshal, and two men with the last name of Crockett. There were soldiers of fortune, policemen, gamblers, miners, and society clubmen. Roosevelt called it "as typical an American regiment as ever marched or fought."

Although Roosevelt might have commanded the First Volunteer Cavalry unit (and later did), he chose to be second in command to his friend Colonel Leonard Wood. He knew his limitations as a military commander. Roosevelt wore a special khaki uniform with bright yellow trim that he ordered from Brooks Brothers.

More than 1,000 men were recruited, 565 of whom went to Cuba with Roosevelt. To their surprise, the cavalrymen (except for Roosevelt) were forced to leave their horses in the United States. In Cuba, the Rough Riders began wryly to call themselves "Wood's Weary Walkers."

Roosevelt with his stalwart Rough Riders.

The Rough Riders trained in San Antonio, Texas, then went by train to Tampa for embarkation. On June 14, 1898, they set sail for Cuba and landed on June 22.

> **❝** I have always been unhappy, most unhappy, that I was not severely wounded in Cuba... in some striking and disfiguring way. **❞**
>
> – THEODORE ROOSEVELT

The Rough Riders fought in two battles in Cuba. The first, on June 24, at Las Guasimas, was Roosevelt's first experience in war. "We lost a dozen men killed or mortally wounded, and sixty severely or slightly wounded," he wrote. "One man was killed as he stood beside a tree with me. Another bullet went through a tree behind which I stood and filled my eyes with bark."

July 1, 1898, was what Roosevelt later called "my crowded hour." On that day, alone on horseback at the front of his loyal Rough Riders, Roosevelt led the famous charge up Kettle Hill, and then nearby San Juan Hill. Journalist Richard Harding Davis reported that Roosevelt "was the most conspicuous figure in the charge." Spanish troops on the heights raked fire down upon the Americans. Roosevelt said his men were mowed down like ninepins. "The Mauser bullets drove in sheets through the trees," he wrote. To one frightened soldier who was holding back, Roosevelt said, "Are you afraid to stand up when I am on horseback?"

**T**heodore Roosevelt killed a Spanish soldier using a revolver that had been salvaged from the sunken battleship *Maine*.

Years later, Roosevelt said, "I have always been unhappy, most unhappy, that I was not severely wounded in Cuba... in some striking and disfiguring way." That's Theodore Roosevelt!

The Americans, including the Rough Riders, won a stunning victory. Spain ceded to the United States temporary control over Cuba and indefinite colonial authority over Puerto Rico, Guam, and the Philippines.

**S**uddenly, the United States had an empire. And Theodore Roosevelt was a national hero.

The princess and Theodore Rex in a moment of mutual admiration.

"The fact of my possessing a snake, as well as sundry happenings such as motoring alone with another girl 'all the way from Newport to Boston without a chaperon' had been chronicled in the papers. A letter came from Father that scorched the paper on which it was written. It enumerated the iniquities that I had committed, and my sins of omission too—that I had all but stopped writing to the family, that I did not appear to have a particle of affection for any of them, that I thought only of my own pleasure. It commented sternly on my general character, or lack of it. I answered him promptly and no doubt promised to mend my ways, but I regret that in a temper at being interfered with, I burnt his letter."

Alice Roosevelt Longworth
*Crowded Hours*

# ROOSEVELT AND PRINCESS ALICE

Theodore Roosevelt had six children, one with his first wife Alice Hathaway Lee Roosevelt and five with his second wife Edith Carow Roosevelt. They were all lively and rambunctious children, but it was his oldest daughter Alice who became an American legend.

Alice Roosevelt Longworth was born on February 12, 1884, in New York City. Her mother Alice died just two days later of Bright's disease. Raised first by Roosevelt's sister Bamie, Alice was returned to Roosevelt's care when he remarried late in 1886. Partly because her father absolutely refused to talk about her mother, or even to mention her name, and partly because Edith's five children came in rapid (and chaotic) succession, Alice never felt that she had equal status in her father's heart.

Alice was just 17 years old when Roosevelt assumed the presidency in September 1901, after the assassination of William McKinley.

Alice rebelled in every way she knew how. She smoked. When the president declared that no child of his would ever smoke in the White House, she climbed up on the roof and smoked there. She drank. She tore around the Eastern seaboard in a jalopy, often racing at 25 miles per hour! She aligned herself with the smart set—rich, idle, sophisticated socialites, the kind of people TR despised, who regarded themselves as too exclusive to sully themselves in the gritty political reforms that TR espoused. She flirted shamelessly, sometimes with men who were not strictly eligible. She appeared at White House dinners carrying her green snake Emily Spinach, named after an exceptionally thin aunt.

> *I can either run the country or I can attend to Alice, but I cannot possibly do both.*
>
> — THEODORE ROOSEVELT

She was a constant trial to TR and long-suffering Edith, who did everything she could to love Alice and restrain her many excesses.

In 1906 Alice married Ohio Republican Congressman Nicholas Longworth in a splendid White House wedding. As she prepared to leave, Edith kissed her and said, "We're glad you're going, you've been nothing but trouble."

Even so, Roosevelt loved his daughter dearly, saw a fair amount of himself in her, and relied on her as a political adviser and goodwill ambassador. In 1905 TR sent her

Alice Roosevelt at about 18 years old, during the White House years.

along with Secretary of War William Howard Taft, 23 congressmen, and seven senators on an "Imperial Cruise" to Japan, Hawaii, and China. She made headlines wherever she went. She attended sumo wrestling, met the emperor of Japan and the empress dowager of China. On the cruise to Japan she shocked everyone by jumping fully clothed into the ship's pool and convincing a flummoxed congressman to follow suit.

Back home, after she had done something particularly egregious, the president's close friend, Owen Wister, asked TR if he couldn't do something about Alice. The president snapped, "I can either run the country or I can attend to Alice, but I cannot possibly do both."

Alice lived until February 20, 1980. She was a sharply opinionated Washington socialite and power broker who had lunch with every president of her lifetime.

Her motto: "If you haven't got anything good to say about anyone, come and sit by me!"

Edith Roosevelt was a strong, intelligent, and extremely private First Lady.

"Oh, sweetest of all sweet girls, last night I dreamed that I was with you, that our separation was but a dream; and when I waked up it was almost too hard to bear. Well, one must pay for everything; you have made the real happiness of my life; and so it is natural and right that I should constantly [be] more and more lonely without you... Do you remember when you were such a pretty engaged girl, and said to your lover 'no Theodore, that I cannot allow'? Darling, I love you so. In a very little over four months I shall see you, now. When you get this three fourths of the time will have gone. How very happy we have been these twenty-three years!"

Roosevelt to Edith from Africa
1910

# ROOSEVELT AND HIS SECOND WIFE EDITH

Edith Carow was Theodore Roosevelt's childhood sweetheart. It was widely assumed that they would eventually marry. In 1878, when Roosevelt was 19 and Edith was 17, something went wrong in their relationship. They remained friends, but all talk of marriage abruptly ended. Years later Roosevelt explained to his sister Bamie, "Edith and I had very intimate relations; one day there came a break for we both of us had... tempers that were far from being the best. To no soul now living have either of us ever since spoken a word of this."

In fall 1878, Roosevelt fell in love with 17-year-old Alice Hathaway Lee of Boston. He decided instantly that she would become his wife. Although Alice was far less certain, Roosevelt campaigned for her heart with such impetuosity and determination that she eventually agreed to marry him. They were married on October 27, 1880, Roosevelt's 22nd birthday. Edith attended the wedding and, as she put it, danced the soles of her shoes off.

Alice Roosevelt died on February 14, 1884. Roosevelt said the light had gone out of his life forever.

He was wrong.

Although he tried strenuously to avoid it, Roosevelt had several "chance" encounters with Edith in his sister's home during trips to New York. Somehow they rekindled their love. On November 17, 1885, Edith accepted TR's marriage proposal. On December 2, 1886, they were married at St. George's Church of Hanover Square in London, England. TR's best man was a British diplomat he had just met on the voyage from New York, Cecil Spring-Rice. Spring-Rice would later become British Ambassador to the U.S. during Roosevelt's presidency.

Edith was Roosevelt's intellectual equal. She was not quite so voracious a reader as her husband, but she had exquisite literary taste. She was by all accounts a better judge of character than TR and advised him in careful and respectful ways. She was somewhat more class conscious than her husband and more reserved in public. Because she had known Roosevelt from earliest childhood and understood that his exuberance, aggressiveness, talkativeness, and ego were deeply woven into his character, she made few attempts to inhibit him or to try to talk him out of adventures that took him away from her for weeks at a time. When he dominated a

President Roosevelt and his second wife Edith in 1902.

formal dinner conversation even more than usual, she sometimes gave him a certain look, at which he shrank back (momentarily) and said, "Now, Edie, I was just..."

Roosevelt remained actively in love with Edith for the rest of his life. "There is nothing in the world," he wrote, "no possible success, military or political which is worth weighing in the balance for one moment against the happiness that comes to those fortunate enough to make a real love match—a match in which the lover and sweetheart will never be lost in husband and wife."

Roosevelt died on January 6, 1919. Edith lived until September 30, 1948. She survived TR by 29 years.

Ambassador Jusserand with his clothes on.

"While in the White House I always tried to get a couple of hours' exercise in the afternoons—sometimes tennis, more often riding, or else a rough cross-country walk, perhaps down Rock Creek, which was then as wild as a stream in the White Mountains, or on the Virginia side along the Potomac. My companions at tennis or on these rides and walks we gradually grew to style the Tennis Cabinet; and then we extended the term to take in many of my old-time Western friends such as Ben Daniels, Seth Bullock, Luther Kelly, and others who had taken part with me in more serious outdoor adventures than walking and riding for pleasure… Often, especially in the winters and early springs, we would arrange for a point to point walk, not turning aside for anything—for instance, swimming Rock Creek or even the Potomac if it came in our way. Of course under such circumstances we had to arrange that our return to Washington should be when it was dark, so that our appearance might scandalize no one."

*Autobiography*

# ROOSEVELT AND POINT TO POINT

Theodore Roosevelt personified the "hands on" father. There was always a measure of the overgrown boy in his character. His wife Edith said she regarded him as her sixth (and least obedient!) child. Roosevelt loved to camp, hunt, fish, and tramp around with his children. He loved to tell ghost stories around the camp fire and tales of the American frontier.

Long before Roosevelt became the U.S. president, he and his gang of young adventurers invented the game "Point to Point." The idea was to designate something on the far horizon, line up in single file, and then march "point to point" to reach that goal. No deviations were allowed. If

> " We had better strip, so as not to wet our things in the creek. "
>
> — THEODORE ROOSEVELT
> TO AMBASSADOR JUSSERAND

you came to a haystack, the rules required that you climb up and over it. If you came to a house, you knocked on the front door and exited through the back door. If you came to a tree, you climbed it. Point to Point. Anyone who did not have the right stuff was sent home in ignominy.

Roosevelt said the game built character and taught his children to keep their eyes on the goal and overcome obstacles. But it was mostly just bully good fun.

The rambunctious Roosevelts at home.

The most famous episode of Point to Point involved the Washington diplomatic corps. The French Ambassador Jules Jusserand wrote, "I arrived at the White House punctually, in afternoon dress and silk hat, as if we were to stroll in the Tuilleries Garden. Two or three other gentlemen came and we started off at what seemed to me a breakneck pace, which soon brought us out of the city."

Then the fun began. "On reaching the country, the President went pell-mell over the fields, following neither road nor path, always on, on, straight ahead! I was much winded, but I would not give in, nor ask him to slow up, because I had the honor of *la belle France* in my heart."

"At last we came to a bank of a stream, rather wide and too deep to be forded. I sighed with relief, because I thought that now we had reached our goal and would rest a moment and catch our breath before turning homeward. But judge of my horror when I saw the President unbutton his clothes and heard him say, 'We had better strip, so as not to wet our things in the creek.' "

With Gallic reluctance, Jusserand finally "removed my apparel, everything except my lavender kid gloves."

There was no way that Roosevelt was going to let this pass without comment. "The President cast an inquiring look at these as if they, too, must come off, but I quickly forestalled any remark by saying, 'With your permission, Mr. President, I will keep these on; otherwise it would be embarrassing if we should meet ladies.'"

Though Jusserand and the other diplomats did not exactly enjoy Roosevelt's strenuous antics, they never forgot that they had been privileged to know and work with one of the most extraordinary men of the twentieth century.

Roosevelt at Lincoln's tomb at Springfield, Illinois, in 1903.

"He grew to know greatness, but never ease. Success came to him, but never happiness, save that which springs from doing well a painful and a vital task. Power was his, but not pleasure. The furrows deepened on his brow, but his eyes were undimmed by either hate or fear. His gaunt shoulders were bowed, but his steel thews never faltered as he bore for a burden the destinies of his people. His great and tender heart never shrank from giving pain; and the task allotted to him was to pour out like water the life-blood of the young men, and to feel in his every fiber the sorrow of the women. Disaster saddened but never dismayed him. As the red years of war went by they found him ever doing his duty in the present, ever facing the future with fearless front, high of heart, and dauntless of soul. Unbroken by hatred, unshaken by scorn, he worked and suffered for the people. Triumph was his at the last; and barely had he tasted it before murder found him, and the kindly, patient, fearless eyes were closed forever."

Address at Hodgenville, Kentucky
February 12, 1903

# ROOSEVELT AND ABRAHAM LINCOLN

**A**braham Lincoln was Theodore Roosevelt's favorite president.

One of the first photographs we have of Roosevelt was taken during Lincoln's funeral cortege in New York City on April 25, 1865. As the procession moved slowly up Broadway past the corner of 14th Street, Theodore (then known as Teedie) and his brother Elliott can be seen peering out of the second story window of his grandfather Cornelius' mansion.

**R**oosevelt was six years old. It was the beginning of a lifelong admiration.

Roosevelt admired Lincoln for several reasons. First, he held the Union together through its greatest national crisis. Second, he freed the slaves. Third, Lincoln was not afraid to stretch his executive authority to save the Union, even when that required extra-constitutional measures such as the suspension of habeas corpus. Roosevelt believed that the president has broad undefined powers to preserve and protect America and to advance the equality and happiness of the American people—powers that must not be hamstrung by a fastidious adherence to the letter of the Constitution. Fourth, he admired Lincoln as a family man. Fifth, he shared Lincoln's commitment to the development of the American West.

**R**oosevelt also believed Lincoln, who was criticized for the slow and compromising path he took to the Emancipation Proclamation (January 1, 1863), had done more to ease the plight of African Americans than any other American. Roosevelt despised righteous moral absolutists who stood on the periphery of American life and sat in judgment of those who were, in his famous words, "actually in the arena."

Roosevelt also admired Lincoln's belief that the common people of America were more important than the larger-than-life capitalists who sometimes provided them employment.

Of Lincoln TR wrote, "It is impossible to conceive of a man farther removed from baseness, farther removed from corruption, from mere self-seeking; but it is also impossible to conceive of a man of more sane and healthy mind—a man less under the influence of that fantastic and diseased morality which makes a man in this workaday world refuse to do what is possible because he cannot accomplish the impossible."

On the eve of Roosevelt's inauguration in 1904, Secretary of State John Hay gave him a remarkably thoughtful gift. Hay had been a friend of Roosevelt's father Thee. For a very long time he had regarded Theodore Roosevelt as an undisciplined and even

Roosevelt and his brother Elliott watch Lincoln's funeral procession in New York City, 1865.

reckless young man who spoke before he thought and frequently waded into controversies, including delicate international disputes, without having a strategy for anything but total victory. Serving as TR's secretary of state and cleaning up after the impulsive president had been for Hay something of a trial.

**E**ven so, the world-weary Hay found it impossible not to admire and even love Theodore Roosevelt. Knowing of TR's adoration of the 16th president, Hay gave the president a ring that contained a strand of Lincoln's hair. In the accompanying note, Hay wrote, "You are one of the men who most thoroughly understand and appreciate Lincoln."

Needless to say, Roosevelt was profoundly moved by Hay's gift.

> **"It is impossible to conceive of a man farther removed from baseness, farther removed from corruption, from mere self-seeking."**
>
> – THEODORE ROOSEVELT ABOUT ABRAHAM LINCOLN

How the other half lives, 1907.

"The midnight trips that Riis and I took enabled me to see what the Police Department was doing, and also gave me personal insight into some of the problems of city life. It is one thing to listen in perfunctory fashion to tales of over-crowded tenements, and it is quite another actually to see what that overcrowding means, some hot summer night, by even a single inspection during the hours of darkness. There was a very hot spell one midsummer while I was Police Commissioner, and most of each night I spent walking through the tenement-house districts and visiting police stations to see what was being done. It was a tragic week. We did everything possible to alleviate the suffering. Much of it was heartbreaking, especially the gasping misery of the little children and of the worn-out mothers."

*Autobiography*

# HAROUN AL ROOSEVELT

Theodore Roosevelt was named New York City Police Commissioner in 1895. He threw himself into the work and was immediately voted president of the commission.

Aware that the New York Police force was regarded as the most corrupt in America, Roosevelt set out to accomplish four things. He wanted to clean up the corruption, modernize the force, and enforce all laws on the books. And, of course, he sought to keep himself in the headlines.

Roosevelt installed telephones in the precincts. He created a unique bicycle squad to ease city traffic. He replaced the force's motley sidearms with standardized pistols. He gave service medals to officers who showed special merit. He did everything he could to root out cronyism and the selling of positions on the force for bribes. He raised job requirements and required annual physical exams.

He had the time of his life—as always.

To make sure that policemen were performing their duties responsibly, Roosevelt began to wander the streets of New York at night, incognito. After putting in a full day of work and dining with colleagues or giving a speech, Roosevelt slipped out into the night, often with reformer friend Jacob Riis, author of *How the Other Half Lives*. He'd push his collar up, pull his hat down over his eyes, and stride out into the most dangerous neighborhoods of the city.

When Roosevelt caught a cop drinking on the beat, sleeping, consorting with prostitutes, or otherwise misbehaving, he questioned him without always identifying himself. If the cop responded with respect, Roosevelt frequently just gave him a warning. If cops exhibited defiance or disrespect, Roosevelt revealed himself and ordered them to appear at his office the next morning. This usually was enough to bring about the intended reform of behavior.

The *Commercial Advertiser* dubbed one of his midnight excursions "A Bagdad Night." The sub-headlines went on to report: "Roosevelt in the Role of Haroun Alraschid. Police Caught Napping. None Knew the Commissioner: All Were Insolent."

The Islamic leader Haroun al Rashid, also known as Aaron the Just (786-809 CE), became Caliph at the age of 21. He was so eager to make sure his subjects were being treated justly by Baghdad government officials that he often wandered the streets at night in disguise. He and his fabulous court are immortalized in *The Thousand and One Nights*.

Haroun al Roosevelt

Roosevelt regarded each office that he held as potentially his last.

Word circulated through New York City that the flash of Roosevelt's oversized white teeth in the night was enough to strike terror into the hearts of even hardened cops. A popular newspaper cartoon revealed a drunken officer panicking after merely spotting a display of spectacles and dentures in a shop window.

Soon vendors began to take advantage of Police Commissioner Roosevelt's celebrity. A grateful and amused public began to purchase whistles fashioned in the shape of a large set of teeth.

Eventually Roosevelt came into conflict with several fellow commissioners. Just at the time things were becoming intolerable, President William McKinley appointed him assistant secretary of the Navy.

One great episode of his life was over. A much more dramatic one was about to begin.

Reform and righteousness were identical for Roosevelt.

"Any man who studies the social condition of the poor knows that liquor works more ruin than any other one cause. He knows also, however, that it is simply impracticable to extirpate the habit entirely, and that to attempt too much often merely results in accomplishing too little; and he knows, moreover, that for a man alone to drink whiskey in a barroom is one thing, and for men with their families to drink light wines or beer in respectable restaurants is quite a different thing."

*Atlantic Monthly*
September 1897

# ROOSEVELT AND THE SUNDAY CLOSING LAW

For two years (1895-97) Theodore Roosevelt served as a police commissioner of New York City. He did everything he could to clean up the force, which was regarded as the most corrupt in America.

Roosevelt believed laws should be enforced even when they were unpopular. Lax enforcement lowered respect for the idea of law, he argued, and led to bribes and other forms of police corruption.

New York's Sunday Excise Law had been on the books for 38 years. It forbade the sale of liquor on Sunday. It was rarely enforced. Roosevelt believed the New York Legislature should never have passed a law it had no interest in enforcing. The best way to get it repealed was to enforce it to the letter.

On June 10, 1895, Roosevelt instructed police officers to "rigidly enforce" the closing of saloons from midnight Saturday to midnight Sunday. "No matter if you think the law is a bad one," Roosevelt said, "you must see that your men carry out your orders to the letter."

Roosevelt chose to enforce the Sunday closing law partly to root out police corruption. He knew cops routinely took bribes to "look the other way" when saloons continued their Sunday business.

In 1895 there were as many as 15,000 saloons in New York. For thousands of immigrants, Sunday was their only day of rest and social satisfaction after six grueling days of labor. Saloons were, historian Kathleen Dalton has written, "the heart of sociability in a tough city."

Roosevelt's crusade was exceedingly unpopular. He was denounced and accused of hypocrisy for enforcing the laws in saloons while gentlemen in elite social clubs had free access to liquor seven days a week.

Roosevelt was not one to shrink from controversy. He wore his sudden unpopularity as a badge of honor. He faced critics at a meeting of German Americans at the Good Government Club on July 16, 1895. His forthrightness turned the hostile crowd into allies. His job, he told the disgruntled crowd, was not to interpret the law, but to enforce it. The Excise Law, he said, was "enforced only against the poor or the honest man and violated with impunity by every rich scoundrel and every

> ## "Wo ist der Roosevelt?"
>
> — SHOUTED FROM CROWD AT GERMANTOWN PARADE

How the other half lived in Roosevelt's New York City.

corrupt politician." The applause was long and respectful. A Chicago newspaperman said TR was "undeniably the biggest man in New York, if not the most interesting man in public life."

On September 25, the United Societies for Liberal Sunday Laws staged a protest parade through New York's Germantown. In a spirit of contempt, the organizers sent TR an invitation. To their surprise, Roosevelt showed up at the reviewing stand. An estimated 30,000 marchers passed by in leather trousers and Bismarck helmets. In one wagon, a pretty German girl was draped in black—the grieving Goddess of Liberty. Roosevelt's attentiveness and good humor led one observer to say it seemed "as if the whole affair were in his honor."

Finally, a man in the crowd, hearing that Roosevelt was present, shouted up in anger, *"Wo ist der Roosevelt?"* (So where is this Roosevelt?) With his excited falsetto, Roosevelt leaned forward and shouted, "Hier bin ich!" (Here I am!)

Everyone laughed heartily and fell in love with Roosevelt, in spite of everything.

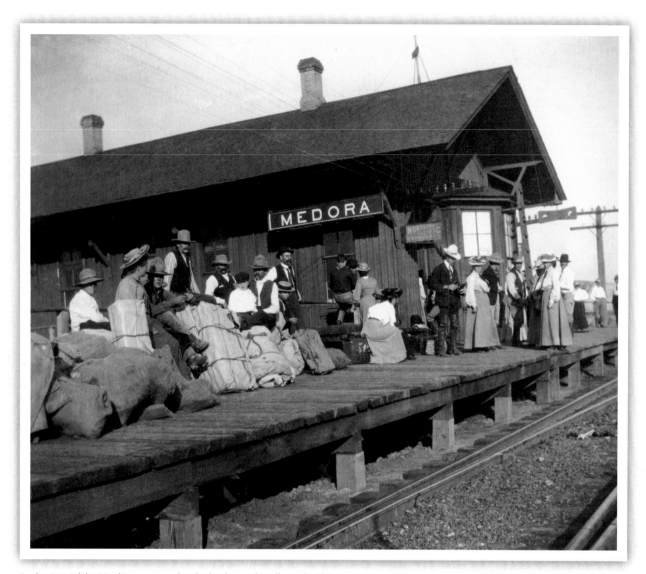

By the time Edith visited in 1890, Medora had a depot. The village of Little Missouri was gone.

"I have rarely seen Edith enjoy anything more than she did the six days at my ranch, and the trip through the Yellowstone Park; and she looks just as well and pretty and happy as she did four years ago when I married her—indeed I sometimes almost think she looks if possible even sweeter and prettier, and she is as healthy as possible, and so young looking and slender to be the mother of those two sturdy little scamps, Ted and Kermit."

To Gertrude Carow (Edith's mother)
October 18, 1890

# EDITH VISITS THE ELKHORN RANCH

Theodore Roosevelt invested in his two Dakota Territory ranches before he married his childhood sweetheart Edith Carow in 1886. Edith was TR's second wife. His first, Alice Hathaway Lee, died two days after giving birth to TR's oldest child Alice.

At the time Roosevelt chose the location of his second ranch, the Elkhorn (35 miles north of Medora), in June 1884, he was not sure he would ever return to New York. He had come west to bury himself in grief, to lead the strenuous life on one of the last American frontiers on the principle that "black care seldom sits behind a rider whose pace is fast enough."

Edith Carow Roosevelt

After he married Edith Carow in December 1886, TR wanted her to see the landscape of the Dakota badlands, where he had undergone the most important physical and spiritual transformation of his life. It wasn't until 1890 that he finally managed to get Edith to North Dakota. By then he was a U.S. Civil Service Commissioner living most of the time in Washington, D.C.

The Roosevelt party arrived by train on September 2, 1890. Besides Edith and TR, the party consisted of Roosevelt's two sisters Bamie (Anna) and Corinne, Corinne's husband Douglas Robinson, TR's friend Bob Ferguson, and the son of Henry Cabot Lodge, George (Bay) Lodge.

Roosevelt, an amateur photographer, took this picture of the Elkhorn Ranch.

Things didn't start out well. It was raining cats and dogs when they arrived. By the time the travelers got from the depot to Joe Ferris' store in Medora, Edith, a woman of great refinement, was covered with "glutinous slime." The party rested for a short time at Ferris' store, then set off for the Elkhorn. The men rode horses while the ladies rode in a horse-drawn wagon.

The road was primitive, to put it lightly. According to Corinne, who wrote a splendid account of the journey, the party crossed the Little Missouri fully 23 times in the 35-mile journey. Corinne said the riverbanks were so steep that the wagon had to plunge down one bank in order to work up enough momentum to careen up the other side!

Edith cheered up when she saw her husband's rustic but well-made cabin, hidden deep in the most beautiful region of the Dakota badlands. She climbed a butte. She chased prairie dogs. She rode a horse called Wire Fence. And TR's plucky sister Corinne attempted to "wrastle" a calf.

After a week in the Dakota badlands, the party moved on to Yellowstone National Park, another of TR's favorite places. He wrote to Edith's mother: "I have rarely seen Edith enjoy anything more than she did the six days at my ranch… and she looks just as well and pretty and happy as she did four years ago when I married her."

> *" Black care seldom sits behind a rider whose pace is fast enough. "*
>
> — THEODORE ROOSEVELT

It was Edith's only trip to the badlands. It was also one of the last times TR spent more than a day or two in his beloved Dakota.

When Boss Platt grew tired of TR in New York, he kicked him
upstairs—towards the presidency.

"It was given to President McKinley to take the foremost place in our
political life at a time when our country was brought face to face with
problems more momentous than any whose solution we have ever
attempted, save only in the Revolution and in the Civil War; and it was
under his leadership that the nation solved these mighty problems aright.
Therefore he shall stand in the eyes of history not merely as the first man
of his generation, but as among the greatest figures in our national life,
coming second only to the men of the two great crises in which the Union
was founded and preserves."

Banquet in honor of the birthday of McKinley
January 27, 1903

# HOW ROOSEVELT BECAME PRESIDENT

"**I** rose like a rocket," he later wrote. Theodore Roosevelt was an ambitious and extraordinarily talented man with a strong commitment to public service. From an early age, the arc of his career pointed him almost inevitably towards the White House.

He got there through the back door.

Roosevelt's heroics in Cuba (1898) propelled him into the governorship of New York. The Republican bosses of New York were perfectly willing for TR to be governor, so long as he played the game according to long-established rules of cronyism and complacency in the face of corruption, so long as he did not press his reforms too strenuously.

Roosevelt could not play by those rules. He soon exhausted the patience of Republican bosses, particularly Thomas C. Platt, the "Easy Boss." When TR indicated his determination to stand for re-election in 1900, Platt and his advisers decided to get rid of the reformer and maverick by nominating him for the vice presidency of the United States. That way, he would have to leave New York, and his political career would effectively be stalled.

"**I** really do not see that there is anything in the Vice-Presidency for me," Roosevelt wrote at the end of 1899. "In the Vice-Presidency I could do very little; whereas as Governor I can accomplish a great deal."

A later vice president, John Nance Garner, famously said the office was "not worth a bucket of warm piss." Roosevelt would become the first vice president ever elected to a full term as president, after ascending to that office upon the death of his predecessor.

Most people saw Roosevelt's march to the presidency as inevitable. Many feared it.

In spite of misgivings, Roosevelt let himself be nominated for the vice presidency at the Republican National Convention, June 19-21, 1900, in Philadelphia. Incumbent president William McKinley handily won re-election in 1900 (over William Jennings Bryan). Roosevelt presided over the United States Senate for precisely five days before the spring 1901 adjournment. "The Vice Presidency," he wrote, "is an utterly anomalous office (one which I think ought to be abolished)."

**R**oosevelt was on a speaking tour of Vermont when he received the news that McKinley had been shot on September 6, 1901, in Buffalo, New York, by an anarchist named Leon Czolgosz. He hastened to McKinley's side. The president seemed likely to recover, so Roosevelt joined his family for a vacation outing in the Adirondack Mountains of upstate New York.

He was climbing down a trail at Mount Marcy when he saw a messenger jogging up towards him. "I felt at once that he had bad news."

Roosevelt hastened to Buffalo. The president was already dead. In borrowed attire, in the home of his friend Ansley Wilcox, he took the oath of office to become the 26th president of the United States. It was September 14, 1901.

> "**The Vice Presidency is an utterly anomalous office.**"
>
> — THEODORE ROOSEVELT

To his closest friend Henry Cabot Lodge, Roosevelt wrote, "It is a dreadful thing to come into the Presidency in this way; but it would be far worse to be morbid about it. Here is the task, and I have got to do it to the best of my ability."

TR said no man ever enjoyed being president as much as he did.

"I have a definite philosophy about the Presidency. I think it should be a very powerful office, and I think the President should be a very strong man who uses without hesitation every power that the position yields; but because of this very fact I believe that he should be sharply watched by the people, held to a strict accountability by them, and that he should not keep the office too long."

To Henry Cabot Lodge
July 19, 1908

# ROOSEVELT'S FIRST DAY IN THE WHITE HOUSE

Theodore Roosevelt was an accidental president. He ascended to the highest office when President William McKinley was assassinated in September 1901. Roosevelt took the oath of office on the afternoon of September 14, 1901, at a private home in Buffalo, New York. In the days that followed, Roosevelt attended McKinley's funeral in Canton, Ohio. He made sure that McKinley's grief-stricken wife Ida had all the time she needed to vacate the executive mansion.

Monday, September 23, 1901, was Roosevelt's first day in the White House. He had been president for just over a week. Edith was still at Sagamore Hill, packing up and supervising the family's move to Washington, D.C. The suddenness of McKinley's exit, coupled with the fact that the Roosevelts had six children and the school year was well underway, made Edith's support role a difficult one.

Theodore Roosevelt was only 42 years old at the time of his ascension. He remains the youngest president in the history of the United States.

Roosevelt did not want to spend his first night in the White House alone, so he asked his two sisters Corinne and Anna (Bamie) and their husbands to dine with him.

Sometime during the course of his first day in the White House, Roosevelt realized that it was one day after his late father's 70th birthday. Theodore Roosevelt, Sr., died in 1878, when his son was a sophomore at Harvard. He was just 46 years old.

Roosevelt virtually worshipped his father. "My father, Theodore Roosevelt, was the best man I ever knew . . . but he was the only man of whom I was ever really afraid," TR wrote in his *Autobiography*. Virtually everything Roosevelt ever did was intended to please his father, even in the decades following his death. When he led the Rough Riders in Cuba, he was seeking as much to vindicate the Roosevelt name as to perform his national duty in a time of war. Roosevelt, Sr., had hired a proxy to fight for him in the Civil War, a sensible move that his son regarded as a stain on the family's honor.

> " In any moment of decision, the best thing you can do is the right thing, the next best thing is the wrong thing, and the worst thing you can do is nothing. "
>
> — THEODORE ROOSEVELT

Roosevelt signs papers in the White House. Notice the roses.

Over dinner on September 23, 1901, President Roosevelt was in a reflective and nostalgic mood, "I have realized it as I signed various papers all day long, and I feel it is a good omen that I begin my duties in this house on this day. I feel my father's hand on my shoulder, as if there were a special blessing over the life I am to lead here."

At the end of the meal, the White House staff, in accordance with long-standing custom, gave each male table guest a flower along with his coffee. As the yellow saffronia rose was placed in front of the new president of the United States, he flushed.

"Isn't that strange!" Roosevelt said. "This is the rose we all connect with our father." Roosevelt's sisters confirmed that the saffronia rose was their father's favorite, that he pruned those roses with special care at the family home on Twentieth Street in New York.

The president spoke, "I think there is a blessing connected with this."

A new era in American history had begun.

Archie Roosevelt on his Shetland pony Algonquin in front of the new White House offices, 1903.

"Yesterday morning at a quarter of seven all the children were up and dressed and began to hammer at the door of their mother's and my room, in which their six stockings, all bulging out with queer angles and rotundities, were hanging from the fireplace. So their mother and I got up, shut the window, lit the fire, taking down the stockings, of course, put on our wrappers and prepared to admit the children. But first there was a surprise for me, also for their good mother, for Archie had a little Christmas tree of his own which he had rigged up with the help of one of the carpenters in a big closet; and we all had to look at the tree and each of us got a present off of it. There was also one present each for Jack the dog, Tom Quartz the kitten, and Algonquin the pony, whom Archie would not more think of neglecting than I would neglect his brothers and sister."

To James A. Garfield, Jr.
December 26, 1902

# LIFE IN THE ROOSEVELT WHITE HOUSE

When he was about to leave the presidency in March, 1909, Theodore Roosevelt wrote, "No man ever enjoyed being president more than I did… I don't think any family has enjoyed the White House more than we have."

The Roosevelts were the first real presidential family in the White House since Abraham Lincoln. And they made the most of it.

The stories are legendary. Alice Roosevelt, forbidden by her father to smoke in the White House, climbed up on the roof and smoked there. The children threw water balloons down onto the heads of Secret Service agents. Quentin and his "White House Gang" pelted the portraits of previous presidents with spitballs—for which they were severely rebuked by the current president. The younger children slid down White House banisters on trays borrowed from the kitchen. Nightly pillow fights were standard. The children careened around the wooden floors on roller skates and lurched about the building on stilts.

When Archie was ill, the youngest of the Roosevelt children, Quentin, decided that his brother would get better faster if he could spend a few minutes with his pony Algonquin. Quentin made this possible by taking Algonquin up to the family quarters in the White House elevator.

The Roosevelts maintained a veritable White House menagerie. The family pets included Algonquin, Alice's garter snake named Emily Spinach, at least ten dogs (mostly terriers, but also a Pekingese named Manchu and a Saint Bernard named Rollo), cats named Tom Quartz and Slippers, a piebald rat named Jonathan, a herd of Guinea pigs, Baron Spreckle the Hen, a one-legged rooster, a Macaw named Eli Yale, a bear named

Roosevelt and "Josiah" the badger in Sharon Springs, Kansas, May 1903.

Jonathan Edwards, and a parrot that had been trained to say "Hurray for Roosevelt!"

> " The credit belongs to the man who is actually in the arena, whose face is marred by dust and sweat and blood. "
>
> — THEODORE ROOSEVELT

Beginning in the summer of 1903, the menagerie also included Josiah the badger, a gift to Roosevelt from a little girl in Sharon Springs, Kansas, on May 3, 1903.

The Roosevelts entertained lavishly during their tenure. The president set the world record for most handshakes in a single day on January 1, 1907. His total of 8,513 handshakes was not beaten anywhere in the world until 1977.

During Roosevelt's tenure, the White House became a serious venue for the arts for the first time in

American history, thanks largely to Roosevelt's cultured wife Edith. The Roosevelts hosted the first White House program by a famous concert pianist, the first musicale devoted to a single opera, and the first performance on a clavichord. One of the most remarkable moments of the Roosevelt years occurred on January 15, 1904, when 28-year-old Spanish cellist Pablo Casals performed in the White House. More than a half century later, Casals returned to the White House to perform for President and Jacqueline Kennedy. Alice Roosevelt Longworth was present on both occasions.

Beginning in 1902, the Roosevelts also remodeled the White House, which TR said reminded him of a second-rate Victorian hotel. Edith Roosevelt took the lead, removing the Victorian encrustations and returning the house as much as possible to its Federal-period roots with some Georgian elements. The Roosevelts also added the first West Wing.

One more thing:

It was Theodore Roosevelt who decided, in 1901, that the president's residence would thereafter always be officially known as the White House.

Booker T. Wahington's reply to the dinner invitation that got Roosevelt into so much trouble.

"In this incident I deserve no particular credit. When I asked Booker T. Washington to dinner I did not devote very much thought to the matter one way or the other. I respect him greatly and believe in the work he has done. I have consulted so much with him it seemed to me that it was natural to ask him to dinner to talk over this work, and the very fact that I felt a moment's qualm on inviting him because of his color made me ashamed of myself and made me hasten to send the invitation. I did not think of its bearing one way or the other, either on my own future or on anything else. As things have turned out, I am very glad that I asked him, for the clamor aroused by the act makes me feel as if the act was necessary."

To Albion Winegar Tourgee
November 8, 1901

# GUESS WHO'S COMING TO DINNER

It happened innocently enough. Roosevelt had been president of the United States for just a month. Hearing that the founder of the Tuskegee Institute, Booker T. Washington, was in town, Roosevelt invited him to have dinner with the family. No African American had been invited to dinner in the 101-year history of the White House.

Booker T. Washington (1856-1918) was a black educator, civil rights leader, and author. Washington espoused cooperation with the white majority and a gradualist approach to black rights. He and Roosevelt had been friends for many years.

The dinner occurred at 7:30 p.m. on October 16, 1901. By 2 a.m. the next morning, the Associated Press issued the following statement: "Booker T. Washington, of Tuskegee, Alabama, dined with the President last evening."

Then all hell broke loose.

The *Memphis Scimitar* in Tennessee spoke for much of the American South. "The most damnable outrage which has ever been perpetrated by any citizen of the United States was committed yesterday by the President, when he invited a n— to dine with him at the White House... No Southern woman with a proper self-respect would now accept an invitation to the White House, nor would President Roosevelt be welcomed today in Southern homes."

Other newspapers called Roosevelt, "A RANK NEGROPHILIST"..."OUR COON-FLAVORED

President Roosevelt and Booker T. Washington at the Tuskegee Institute, 1905.

PRESIDENT" ... a promoter of the "MINGLING AND MONGRELIZATION" of the Anglo-Saxon race.

Senator Benjamin R. Tillman of South Carolina said, "The action of President Roosevelt in entertaining that n— will necessitate our killing a thousand n—s in the South before they will learn their place again."

---

**"Your act in honoring Washington was a masterly stroke of statesmanship..."**

— A ROOSEVELT SUPPORTER

---

The *Richmond News* in Virginia intoned, "At one stroke, and by one act, he has destroyed the kindly, warm regard and personal affection for him which were growing up fast in the south. Hereafter ... it will be impossible to feel, as we were beginning to feel, that he is one of us."

The *Richmond Times* tried to follow the dinner invitation to what it regarded as its logical conclusion. "It means that the President is willing that negroes shall mingle freely with whites in the social circle—that white women may receive attentions from negro men; it means that there is no racial reason in his opinion why whites and blacks may not marry and intermarry."

A southern white pastor wrote, "The whole South has not been so deeply moved in twenty years."

All this from supper!

The national response was not all negative, however.

One citizen wrote to the president, "Your act in honoring Washington was a masterly stroke of statesmanship—worthy of the best minds this country has produced."

Roosevelt was dumbfounded by the storm of protest. He refused to apologize or explain his actions. TR privately declared that he would invite anyone he wished to the White House, and if people didn't like it they could impeach him or retire him at the next election.

Even so, he never invited an African American to a White House dinner again.

Roosevelt and America's most famous journalist Richard Harding Davis, 1898.

"I want to let in light and air, but I do not want to let in sewer-gas. If a room is fetid and the windows are bolted I am perfectly contented to knock a hole into the drain-pipe. In other words, I feel that the man who in a yellow newspaper or in a yellow magazine makes a ferocious attack on good men or even attacks bad men with exaggeration or for things they have not done, is a potent enemy of those of us who are really striving in good faith to expose bad men, and drive them from power. I disapprove of the whitewash-brush quite as much as of mud-slinging."

To Ray Stannard Baker
April 9, 1906

# ROOSEVELT AND THE PRESS

Theodore Roosevelt had a genius for getting publicity. He led a life of adventure on four continents, wore colorful clothing, and was America's first cowboy president. Whatever he said, even if it was merely a platitude, he said with such force and directness that newspapers could not resist reporting it. At every turn of events, he regarded himself as the one righteous leader in a battle that rose to the proportions of Armageddon. Even so, TR was an immensely likeable man, even to his enemies.

President Roosevelt gave reporters a permanent pressroom inside the White House, including telephones (invented 1876). He held forth freely before his favorite reporters weekdays at 1 p.m. while he was being shaved. Roosevelt was perhaps the first president to master the news leak and the trial balloon. He gave the most "reliable" reporters off-the-record information with the warning, "If you even hint where you got it... I'll say you are a damned liar."

Roosevelt created what he called the Ananias Club, named for a member of the first Christian community who dropped dead after lying to the apostle Peter about the extent of his wealth (Acts 4-5). Reporters consigned to the Ananias Club (for writing anything that Roosevelt found truly objectionable) lost their privileged access to the White House.

When Jesse Carmichael of the *Boston Herald* filed a story about the Roosevelt children chasing the Thanksgiving turkey all over White House grounds and plucking feathers from its flanks, Roosevelt flew into a rage. Carmichael was sentenced to the Ananias Club,

The press loved Theodore Roosevelt, and Roosevelt (usually) loved the press.

of course, but the wrathful president actually attempted to stop the U.S. Weather Bureau from sharing storm information with the city of Boston. The *Herald* wisely apologized, if only to save the city.

> " If you even hint where you got it...I'll say you are a damned liar. "
>
> — THEODORE ROOSEVELT

Roosevelt's dramatic life made for perfect copy. According to historian Edmund Morris, "TR was the first president to realize that big deeds, human interest stories, and dramatic moments sold presidents and their policies to the voters. His well-planned hunts, his trip to Panama, his excursion in a submarine, even his plan to send the Great White Fleet on a cruise were dramatic presidential publicity stunts that worked."

Roosevelt had a special relationship with two of the great journalists of his time. One was Jacob Riis (1849-1914), a Danish-American photojournalist, reformer, and muckraker. Riis had known Roosevelt from the time he served as police commissioner of New York. He took Commissioner Roosevelt into the most impoverished neighborhoods so he could see "how the other half lived."

The other journalist was Finley Peter Dunne (1867-1936), who wrote under the pseudonym of Irish immigrant Mr. Dooley. Dunne was an admirer of Roosevelt, but not an uncritical admirer. His wry observations were frequently read aloud at Roosevelt's cabinet meetings. Roosevelt was a fan, even though he was frequently a target of Dunne's satire. Perhaps the greatest example was "Mr. Dooley's" review of Roosevelt's book *The Rough Riders,* about the Spanish-American War in Cuba. Mr. Dooley liked the book very well, he said, but "if I was him I'd call th' book 'Alone in Cuba.'"

A bear cub in Colorado 1905.

"The preservation of game and of wild life generally—aside from the noxious species—on these reserves is of incalculable benefit to the people as a whole. As the game increases in these national refuges and nurseries it overflows into the surrounding country. Very wealthy men can have private game-preserves of their own. But the average man of small or moderate means can enjoy the vigorous pastime of the chase, and indeed can enjoy wild nature, only if there are good general laws, properly enforced, for the preservation of the game and wild life, and if, furthermore, there are big parks or reserves provided for the use of all our people, like those of the Yellowstone, the Yosemite, and the Colorado."

*A Book-Lover's Holiday in the Open*

# ROOSEVELT AND THE TEDDY BEAR

Theodore Roosevelt did not like to be called Teddy because it was the pet name his first wife Alice had used for him. After her death in 1884, he made it clear that he did not wish to be called Teddy by anyone. But America found the nickname irresistible, and Roosevelt eventually came to terms with it.

In November 1902, President Roosevelt journeyed to the Mississippi River delta country to hunt bear. His guide was an old timer named Holt Collier, a man at home in the pine and swamp country, who had killed more than 3,000 bears in his lifetime. Roosevelt took an instant shine to him.

It proved to be one of Roosevelt's most frustrating hunts. For five days "I never got a shot," Roosevelt reported.

> **I don't think my name will mean much to the bear business, but you're welcome to use it.**
>
> — THEODORE ROOSEVELT

On Friday, November 14, the hunting dogs picked up the scent of a bear. Collier tracked the bear through mud and thickets for several hours. Believing that the bear had somehow escaped, TR and a companion returned to camp for lunch. At 2:30 p.m., Collier and his dogs caught up with an old 235-pound bear. Collier bugled for the president. The bear meanwhile retreated into a slough, surrounded by barking dogs.

The cartoon that launched the career of America's most enduring stuffed animal.

The bear seized one of the dogs and crushed it. Collier lunged in to protect the rest of the dogs and, in the process, struck the bear on the head with the barrel of his rifle. He threw a rope around the bear's neck.

President Roosevelt arrived on the scene to discover a dead dog and a stunned bear tied to a tree.

The hunters cried, "Let the president shoot the bear!" Roosevelt hesitated, then declined. "Put it out of its misery," he demanded. One of the hunters thrust a knife between the bear's ribs.

On Sunday, November 16, the *Washington Post* ran a story about Roosevelt's gesture of good sportsmanship. The president had "refused to make an unsportsmanlike shot," the *Post* reported. The next day the *Post* featured a front page cartoon by Clifford Berryman. The cartoon featured not the large bear that had been stunned, tied to a tree, and knifed to death, but an adorable live bear cub with a rope

around its neck. The caption read, "Drawing the Line in Mississippi."

The cartoon was reprinted across America.

Eventually, Brooklyn toy maker Rose Michtom fashioned two plush bears, adorned with black shoe-button eyes, and displayed them in her store window. When they sold immediately, her husband Morris Michtom wrote to the president in early 1903, asking for permission to sell more such bears and call them Teddy's Bear.

President Roosevelt is said to have written, "I don't think my name will mean much to the bear business, but you're welcome to use it."

And so a frustrating bear hunt led to three enduring results. It inspired one of the most famous political cartoons of American history. It helped to create America's favorite stuffed animal. And, as Edmund Morris writes, it "spawned the most enduring of all Rooseveltian myths."

As time went on, TR took more and more personal credit for the Panama Canal.

"Panama was a great sight. In the first place it was strange and beautiful, with its mass of luxuriant tropic jungle, with the treacherous tropic rivers trailing here and there through it; and it was lovely to see the orchids and brilliant butterflies and the strange birds and snakes and lizards, and finally the strange old Spanish towns and the queer thatch and bamboo huts of the ordinary natives. In the next place it is a tremendous sight to see the work on the canal going on. From the chief engineer and the chief sanitary officer down to the last arrived machinist or time-keeper, the five thousand Americans at work on the Isthmus seemed to me an exceptionally able, energetic lot, some of them grumbling, of course, but on the whole a mighty good lot of men."

To Theodore Roosevelt, Jr.
November 20, 1906

# ROOSEVELT AND THE PANAMA CANAL

Ever since Balboa first gazed from the Isthmus of Panama out at the Pacific Ocean on September 25, 1513, humankind has dreamed of a Panama Canal. The French tried to accomplish the feat in the later nineteenth century, led by the builder of the Suez Canal, Ferdinand de Lesseps. The French failed.

Theodore Roosevelt became president of the United States on September 14, 1901. He decided to get the thing done—or at least started—on his watch.

After a long series of frustrating negotiations with the government of Colombia, the Roosevelt administration welcomed, but did not in fact foment, a revolution in Colombia's northern province Panama. The revolution began on November 3, 1903. The United States recognized the new republic on November 6 with what one historian has called "unseemly haste."

U.S. Secretary of State John Hay and new Panamanian Foreign Minister Bunau-Varilla signed the Panama Canal treaty on November 18, 1903. It gave the United States the right to construct and operate a canal "in perpetuity" for $10 million, an annual payment of $250,000, and a guarantee of Panama's independence.

Roosevelt's extraordinary boldness in handling the canal situation—from his high-handedness on the international stage to his insistence that the Senate pass the canal treaty with uncritical dispatch—generated controversy then and now. His own cabinet officials understood the importance of his personal role in the Panama triumph. At a cabinet meeting, Roosevelt gave an interminable monologue defending the legitimacy of his actions. Attorney General Philander Knox finally said, "Oh, Mr. President, do not let so great an achievement suffer from any taint of legality." TR's sardonic Secretary of War Elihu Root was much more pointed. "You have shown that you were accused of seduction," Root said, "and you have conclusively proved that you were guilty of rape."

Once the Canal Zone was secure, President Roosevelt lost no time in getting construction started. The U.S. Army Corps of Engineers began by waging war against malaria and yellow fever, then excavated the canal and built the six locks that lifted ships up over the 85-foot crest of the isthmus.

In November 1906, Theodore Roosevelt became the first president in American history to leave the United States during his term in office. He and Edith spent three days in Panama during the heaviest rains in a decade. President Roosevelt tramped

Roosevelt digs the Panama Canal himself.

through the mud, inspected barracks, eschewed formal banquets to eat with the largely black work force, clambered up the nearly vertical slopes of the Culebra Cut, and even had the opportunity to get his photograph taken while operating one of the big Bucyrus steam shovels that dug the canal.

Years later, in Berkeley, California, Roosevelt recklessly said, "I took the canal zone." In a typical assertion of executive supremacy, he said, "I... started the canal and then left Congress not to debate the canal, but to debate me... but while the debate goes on the canal does too and they are welcome to debate me as long as they wish, provided that we go on with the canal now."

The Panama Canal opened on August 15, 1914. Unfortunately, Roosevelt did not live long enough to make the transit.

> " I...started the canal and then left Congress not to debate the canal, but to debate me... "
>
> — THEODORE ROOSEVELT

From the pages of *Puck*, an emerging national concern for conservation.

"If in a given community unchecked popular rule means unlimited waste and destruction of the natural resources—soil, fertility, water-power, forests, game, wild life generally—which by right belong as much to subsequent generations as to the present generation, then it is sure proof that the present generation is not yet really fit to exercise the high and responsible privilege of a rule which shall be both by the people and for the people. The term 'for the people' must always include the people unborn as well as the people now alive."

*A Book-Lover's Holidays in the Open*

# THEODORE ROOSEVELT'S CONSERVATION ACHIEVEMENTS

Theodore Roosevelt was one of the great conservationists in American history.

His interest in natural history began at a very early age, but it was not until he lived in the Dakota badlands that his conservation ideas began to coalesce into a lifelong social philosophy.

Even before the disastrous winter of 1886-87, Roosevelt had come to realize that the badlands were being overgrazed, and that a "perfect storm" of drought coupled with a severe winter could precipitate a collapse of the cattle industry. During that legendary winter, approximately 70% of the cattle of the northern plains perished. When he returned to the badlands in April 1887 after his honeymoon in Europe, Roosevelt was shocked by the devastation he surveyed here. He wrote to his sister Bamie that this was first time he could not enjoy his time in the Little Missouri River Valley.

Roosevelt also realized that the great game species of the American West were in danger of disappearing in the wake of for-profit hunting and the pressure of the homestead movement. He got his buffalo in September 1883, but realized that the species needed concerted help if it was to avoid extinction.

Accordingly, Roosevelt joined with his friend George Bird Grinnell in 1887 to create the Boone and Crockett Club, dedicated to scientific game management and to the promotion of national legislation to protect endangered species.

Many of Roosevelt's mature conservation ideas were formulated while he served as governor of New York (1898-1900). During that crucial period in his development as a national political leader, Roosevelt, with the help of Gifford Pinchot, turned his attention to the forests and streams of New York State, and particularly to the Adirondack Mountains.

> " There can be no greater issue than that of conservation in this country. "
> — THEODORE ROOSEVELT

Roosevelt was a fully evolved conservationist by the time he became president of the United States in 1901. He used the "bully pulpit" to maximum advantage during his tenure as president, but he also stretched the Constitution in unprecedented ways in his drive to conserve America's natural resources. He used the executive order to create America's first National Wildlife Refuges (1903), read the Antiquities Act of 1906 in a broad and flexible way, and took advantage of the powers granted to the president in the Forest Reserve Act of 1891 to designate, without consultation with Congress, 150 new National Forests totaling 150 million acres.

The great man in nature's arena – Yosemite 1903.

Roosevelt's conservation record as president is staggering. He added five new National Parks to the system, designated the first 51 National Wildlife Refuges, and tripled the size of the National Forest system. He also established the first 18 National Monuments, beginning with Devils Tower in Wyoming, and designated the first 24 national irrigation projects under the provisions of the Newlands Reclamation Act of 1902.

Altogether President Roosevelt set aside 230 million acres of the public domain for permanent federal protection.

At the end of his remarkable administration, Roosevelt hosted the first-ever National Governors Conference at the White House, the theme of which was conservation.

Much of what Roosevelt understood about conservation was born of his experiences in the American West. Roosevelt's Elkhorn Ranch, 35 miles north of Medora, can rightly be regarded as one of the "sacred places" in the history of American conservation, along with Thoreau's cabin at Walden Pond, and Aldo Leopold's cottage in the lake country of Wisconsin.

President Roosevelt and company before the "Grizzly Giant" in California.

"I have written you about many public matters; now just a line about yourself. As long as I live I shall feel for you a mixture of respect and admiration and of affectionate regard. I am a better man for having known you… and I cannot think of a man in the country whose loss would be a real misfortune to the nation more than yours would be. For seven and a half years we have worked together—and have been altogether better able to work because we have played; and I owe to you a peculiar debt of obligation for a very large part of the achievements of this administration."

To Gifford Pinchot
March 2, 1909

# ROOSEVELT AND GIFFORD PINCHOT

Theodore Roosevelt may have been America's greatest conservationist president. He was a naturalist from a young age. Sometime during his sojourn in the Dakota badlands (1883-87), he realized that the flora and fauna of the American West would need protection to survive the economic onslaught of his time.

Roosevelt's intuitions about the fragility of the environment were deepened by his friendship with Gifford Pinchot, the first professional scientific forester in America. Pinchot (1865-1946) had sterling credentials. Educated at Phillips Exeter Academy and Yale, Pinchot undertook graduate study at the French National Forestry School. He returned from Europe determined to bring scientific forest management to the United States.

Roosevelt and Pinchot met in 1894. In 1899, New York Governor Roosevelt invited Pinchot to visit him in Albany. When Pinchot arrived, he reported that the mansion appeared to be "under ferocious attack from a band of invisible Indians, and the Governor of the Empire State was helping a houseful of children to escape by lowering them out of a second story window on a rope."

In the first of many bonding experiences, the two men boxed, then wrestled in the Governor's Mansion on Eagle Street! That must have been quite a scene—two of the great men of American history, one a future president, the other the most important government conservationist of his era, roughhousing like boys in the governor's residence. "I had the honor of knocking the future President of the United States off of his very solid pins," Pinchot would remember. Roosevelt won the wrestling match, and Pinchot wisely called a halt before the competition got too fierce.

According to historian Douglas Brinkley, "Roosevelt and Pinchot formed an alliance that would have a profound effect on the modern conservation movement."

President McKinley appointed Pinchot Chief U.S. Forester in 1899. Pinchot convinced President Roosevelt to transfer the Division of Forestry from the Department of the Interior to the Department of Agriculture in 1905, on the principle that trees were a sustainable crop that should be managed like other agricultural crops.

> *I had the honor of knocking the future President of the United States off his very solid pins.*
>
> — GIFFORD PINCHOT

Roosevelt and Gifford Pinchot talk the issues on the river steamer *Mississippi*, 1907.

With Pinchot's zealous assistance, Roosevelt added 150 million acres to the National Forest during his seven years as president. In this way, Roosevelt more than tripled the acreage designated as National Forest. In 1907, Oregon Senator Charles Fulton, on behalf of other pro-development western senators, attached a rider to an agricultural appropriations bill that would prevent Roosevelt from designating further National Forests in six northwestern states. Roosevelt knew he had to sign the bill. As a good student of the Constitution, he also knew that he had 10 days between receiving the bill and the time it must be signed. Roosevelt and Pinchot used the interim shrewdly. Together they designated 16 million new acres of National Forest within the states in question. They have been known ever since as the "Midnight Forests."

Roosevelt later wrote, "Gifford Pinchot is the man to whom the nation owes most for what has been accomplished as regards the preservation of the natural resources of our country."

The Bull Moose in his natural element.

"Birds that are useless for the table and not harmful to the farm should always be preserved; and the more beautiful they are, the more carefully they should be preserved. They look a great deal better in the swamps and on the beaches and among the trees than they do on hats. There are certain species in certain localities which it is still necessary to collect; but no really rare bird ought to be shot save in altogether exceptional circumstances and for public museums, and the common birds (which of course should also be placed in public museums) are entirely out of place in private collections; and this applies as much to their eggs and nests as to their skins."

*The Outlook*
September 16, 1911

# THEODORE ROOSEVELT AND PELICAN ISLAND

Theodore Roosevelt loved birds. He loved to look at them, listen to them, study their habits and appearance, and to make lists of all the birds that he had observed. The future president also liked to shoot birds. But he despised the slaughter of birds merely to harvest their feathers for the adornment of ladies' hats.

On March 14, 1903, President Roosevelt signed the executive order that established Pelican Island on the Indian River in Florida as the first federal bird sanctuary.

The story of how this happened is famous in the annals of conservation. Alarmed by the ravages of plume hunters on Pelican Island, a five-acre pinpoint in the Indian River, Roosevelt asked Attorney General Philander Knox if any existing law enabled him to create a federal bird sanctuary. Knox said no such law existed. Then Roosevelt asked a more interesting question, more in keeping with his concept of executive authority. "Is there any law that will prevent me from declaring Pelican Island a Federal Bird Reservation?"

Knox said no. At that the president uttered famous and historically important words: "Very well, then I so declare it."

In the remainder of his time as president, Roosevelt named 50 more bird sanctuaries. Two of them, Stump Lake (1904) and Chase Lake (1908), were designated in North Dakota. The federal bird reservations are now known as National Wildlife Refuges. The total number of refuges nationwide now numbers 584, embracing 150 million acres. North Dakota, with 63, has the

Pelican Island: the first Federal Bird Sanctuary

largest number of National Wildlife Refuges in the United States.

Roosevelt could not have accomplished what he did for American conservation had it not been for hundreds of hard working individuals who fought to save America's wild things in the local arena.

In the case of Pelican Island National Wildlife Refuge, two individuals stand out. First, there was German immigrant Paul Kroegel, who arrived in the area with his father in 1881. Kroegel could look out from the family homestead onto the five-acre mangrove island that housed thousands of brown pelicans and other waterfowl. He used to sail to the island and stand guard with his gun so hat-hunters could not easily decimate the flocks.

> " Very well, then I so declare it. "
> — THEODORE ROOSEVELT

Well-known ornithologist, Frank Chapman, who was curator at the American Museum of Natural

History in New York and a member of the American Ornithologist's Union, visited Pelican Island during the years preceding Roosevelt's executive action. When Chapman discovered that Pelican Island was the last rookery for brown pelicans on the East Coast of Florida, he pledged his support to protect the birds, and successfully lobbied his bird-loving friend Roosevelt, who just happened to be president of the United States.

Individuals like Kroegel and Chapman deserve credit for their hard work, but the federal government would not have become the nation's principal protector of birds had it not been for the passion and enlightenment of the 26th president of the United States Theodore Roosevelt. Ralph Waldo Emerson said an institution is the lengthened shadow of one man. The one man at the heart of the National Wildlife Refuge System was Theodore Roosevelt. His conservation shadow is very long.

Roosevelt plants a tree near San Jose, California, 1903.

"We are just getting to understand what is involved in the preservation of our forests. Not only is an industry at stake which employs more than half a million of men, the lumber industry, but the whole prosperity and development of the West, and indeed ultimately of the entire country, is bound up with the preservation of the forests. Right use of the forests means the perpetuation of our supply both of wood and of water. Therefore we cannot afford to be satisfied with anything short of expert and responsible management of the national reserves and other national forest interests. The forest reserves must be cared for by the best trained foresters to be had, just as the storage reservoirs must be built and maintained by the best engineers."

Letter to the National Irrigation Congress
November 16, 1900

# ROOSEVELT AND THE NATIONAL FORESTS

Theodore Roosevelt loved trees. And he did not like what was happening to the nation's forests during the pell-mell industrialization of the American economy. Looking back on the frontier era of American history, he lamented, "The American had but one thought about a tree, and that was to cut it down."

When the English planted their first permanent colony at Jamestown, Virginia, more than a billion acres of forest graced what became the United States. It was said that in Thomas Jefferson's time, a squirrel could jump from tree to tree all the way from the Chesapeake to the Mississippi River.

According to historian Paul Russell Cutright, "By the end of the nineteenth century, approximately half of this magnificent original stand of timber had been cut, with four-fifths of what remained being in private hands."

Roosevelt did not invent the National Forests, but he made them his own. In 1891 Congress passed the Forest Reserve Act, which authorized presidents to create forest reserves. Presidents Benjamin Harrison, Grover Cleveland, and William McKinley used this power boldly to create 50 million acres of National Forest.

Beginning with his tenure as governor of New York (1899-1900), Roosevelt embraced the forest management approach of his friend and adviser Gifford Pinchot. In an annual message to the New York State Assembly, Governor Roosevelt said, "The fundamental idea of forestry is the perpetuation of forests by use." Roosevelt, like Pinchot, believed forests should be managed for "sustained yield," so that the volume of the annual timber cut would not exceed the capacity of the nation's forests to replace the harvested trees. In accordance with this philosophy, President Roosevelt had the National Forests transferred from the jurisdiction of the Department of Interior to the Department of Agriculture.

During his seven years, 171 days as president, Roosevelt designated a whopping 150 million acres as National Forest. The largest of these, Alaska's Tongass National Forest, established September 10, 1907, now encompasses 17 million acres. On March 2, 1909, just two days before he left the presidency, Roosevelt designated 13 new National Forests in five western states. Imagine if he had served a third term as president.

> *" The American had but one thought about a tree, and that was to cut it down. "*
>
> — THEODORE ROOSEVELT

Roosevelt regarded the great trees of the West as "America's cathedrals."

"Every lover of nature," Roosevelt wrote, "every man who appreciates the majesty and beauty of the wilderness, should strike hands with the far-sighted men who wish to preserve our forests."

Roosevelt understood that forests were not just sources of timber. They were essential to the environmental health of America. They served as "sponges" that stored the meager water resources of the arid lands west of the Mississippi River. In his 1908 Annual Message to Congress, Roosevelt provided the legislative branch with an impassioned lecture on what can happen when a nation permits its forests to be denuded: "What thus has happened in northern China, what has happened in central Asia, in Palestine, in north Africa, in parts of the Mediterranean countries of Europe, will surely happen in our country if we do not exercise that wise foresight which should be one of the chief marks of any people calling itself civilized."

The size and magnificence of America's National Forest System owes more to Theodore Roosevelt than to any other human being.

Two of TR's favorite Americans, John Burroughs and John Muir, ca. 1899.

"Ordinarily, the man who loves the woods and the mountains, the trees, the flowers, and the wild things, has in him some indefinable quality of charm which appeals even to those sons of civilization who care for little outside of paved streets and brick walls. John Muir was a fine illustration of this rule. His was a dauntless soul, and also one brimming over with friendliness and kindliness."

*The Outlook*
January 6, 1915

# ROOSEVELT AND JOHN MUIR

Between April 1 and June 5, 1903, President Theodore Roosevelt undertook a 25-state train trip across America, with a special emphasis on the American West. Partly he wanted to see the country, but with the election of 1904 approaching, he wanted to work the country, too. He gave 262 speeches.

He stopped in Medora (April 7) to greet friends from his earlier days of adventure in the Dakota badlands, to have his photograph taken in the town hall, and to see his old favorite horse, Manitou. In mid-April, he spent two weeks alone in Yellowstone National Park with his naturalist friend John Burroughs.

After entering California on May 7 and working his way through the state, Roosevelt reached the portal of Yosemite National Park on May 15, 1903.

John Muir was waiting for him. Muir (1838-1914) was a Scottish-born American naturalist, writer, wilderness advocate, and founder of the Sierra Club. Muir belonged on the preservationist end of the environmental spectrum, rather than the conservationist position (wise use, sustained yield) espoused by Roosevelt and Chief U.S. Forester Gifford Pinchot. Muir decried unrestrained economic exploitation of the American West. He was a champion of preserving the wilderness of America in its most pristine condition. He disliked the grazing of domesticated animals in the West, once referring to sheep as "hooved locusts."

> "This is the best day of my life!"
>
> — THEODORE ROOSEVELT

Roosevelt had written to the 65-year-old Sierra sage in advance. "I want to drop politics absolutely for four days, and just be out in the open with you."

Without Secret Service detail, Roosevelt and John Muir tramped through Yosemite for three days. Muir created a fireworks display by setting fire to a dead tree. The president was thrilled. They slept under the open sky on a bed of ferns. They talked endlessly—about conservation issues, the flora and fauna of the Sierra, government forest policy, and about San Francisco's insatiable water needs.

With boldness that might have gotten him punched out had he not been the great John Muir, the naturalist asked TR when he would ever get over his infantile need to kill wild things. Roosevelt, for his part, later grumbled that

President Roosevelt and naturalist John Muir in Yosemite National Park, 1903.

Muir did not know how to recognize bird songs. Though they sometimes disagreed about conservation policy, they found common ground in their shared adoration of raw nature. Roosevelt felt that he was "lying in a great solemn cathedral, far vaster and more beautiful than any built by the hands of man."

On the third morning, they woke up under a blanket of four inches of snow. Roosevelt's response: "This is the best day of my life!"

Afterwards, Roosevelt wrote to thank Muir. "I shall never forget our three camps; the first in the solemn temple of the giant sequoias; the next in the snowstorm among the silver firs near the brink of the cliff; and the third on the floor of the Yosemite, in the open valley, fronting the stupendous rocky mass of El Capitan, with the falls thundering in the distance on either hand."

Muir's response to Roosevelt was unequivocal: "I fairly fell in love with him."

The crowd at the cornerstone ceremony, Gardiner, Montana, April 24, 1903.

"The Yellowstone Park is something absolutely unique in the world, so far as I know. Nowhere else in any civilized country is there to be found such a tract of veritable wonderland made accessible to all visitors, where at the same time not only the scenery of the wilderness, but the wild creatures of the Park are scrupulously preserved; the only change being that these same wild creatures have been so carefully protected as to show a literally astounding tameness… This Park was created, and is now administered, for the benefit and enjoyment of the people… The only way that the people as a whole can secure to themselves and their children the enjoyment in perpetuity of what the Yellowstone Park has to give is by assuming the ownership in the name of the nation and by jealously safeguarding and preserving the scenery, the forests, and the wild creatures."

At the laying of the cornerstone at Gardiner, Montana
April 24, 1903

# ROOSEVELT AND YELLOWSTONE NATIONAL PARK

Theodore Roosevelt did not create Yellowstone National Park, but he loved it and helped to save it.

Yellowstone was the world's first National Park. President Ulysses S. Grant signed the Yellowstone bill on March 1, 1872. By the time Roosevelt became president on September 14, 1901, the United States had five National Parks: Yellowstone (1872), Yosemite (1890), Sequoia (1890), General Grant (1890), and Mount Rainier (1899). Roosevelt added five new parks during his tenure: Crater Lake (1902), Wind Cave (1903), Platt (1904), Sullys Hill (1904), Mesa Verde (1906).

Roosevelt first visited Yellowstone National Park in the 1880s. In 1890, after visiting Medora and his Elkhorn Ranch in the badlands of the new state of North Dakota, Roosevelt took his wife Edith and his sisters to Yellowstone. Edith was thrown from her horse, but she still enjoyed her time in the park immensely.

Roosevelt and John Burroughs in Yellowstone National Park.

Roosevelt founded the Boone and Crockett Club with his friend George Bird Grinnell in 1887. The club soon formed a Committee on Parks, "to promote useful and proper legislation towards the enlargement and better government of the Yellowstone National Park." When Yellowstone was established in 1872, Congress had made no provision for policing and protecting the park. The Boone and Crockett Club helped to defeat the plan of the Yellowstone Park Improvement Association to turn the park into a pleasure garden for wealthy tourists. It also helped to defeat plans to run a railroad line through the park, and to have 622 square miles returned to public domain for railroad use.

Roosevelt's most important visit to Yellowstone occurred in April 1903 during his 25-state train trip through the American West. He spent two weeks with his naturalist friend John Burroughs in the park. Burroughs (1837-1921) was a white-bearded, popular natural history essayist who embodied the view that nature was a benign healer of the human spirit.

The 66-year-old Burroughs was not as robust as Roosevelt. He rode into the park—much jostled—in a wagon, while TR rode a horse. When inviting Burroughs to join him at Yellowstone, Roosevelt wrote, "I would see that you endured neither fatigue or hardship." With Roosevelt such vows meant little in practical terms.

Roosevelt would dearly have loved to do some hunting in Yellowstone. He even wrote ahead to arrange for hunting dogs, hoping he could help park officials cull the

President Roosevelt dedicates the gateway arch of Yellowstone National Park.

large mountain lion population. But when his hunting plans threatened to become a public controversy, he backed down. The only animal he killed in the park was a meadow vole, which he harvested merely for the sake of science and sent to his naturalist friend C. Hart Merriam.

Roosevelt spent most of his time in Yellowstone observing and counting elk. Burroughs, awe-struck, called Roosevelt "the most vital man on the continent, if not on the planet, today."

On April 24, 1903, Roosevelt laid the cornerstone at the gateway to Yellowstone National Park at Gardiner, Montana. In his remarks, Roosevelt said, "The Yellowstone Park is something unique in this world, as far as I know. Nowhere else in any civilized country is there to be found such a tract of veritable wonderland, made accessible to all visitors."

> "Nowhere else in any civilized country is there to be found such a tract of veritable wonderland, made accessible to all visitors."
>
> — THEODORE ROOSEVELT

The seven-car presidential train that took Roosevelt to the Grand Canyon.

"In the Grand Canyon, Arizona has a natural wonder which, so far as I know, is in kind absolutely unparalleled throughout the rest of the world. I want to ask you to do one thing in connection with it in your own interest and in the interest of the country—to keep this great wonder of nature as it is now...

We have gotten past the stage, my fellow citizens, when we are to be pardoned if we treat any part of our country as something to be skinned for two or three years for the use of the present generation, whether it is the forest, the water, the scenery. Whatever it is, handle it so that your children's children will get the benefit of it."

Remarks at his first visit to the Grand Canyon
May 6, 1903

# ROOSEVELT AND THE GRAND CANYON

Theodore Roosevelt visited the Grand Canyon for the first time in 1903. He was on a transcontinental train trip that took him to 25 states, including Arizona and California.

The special seven-car presidential train arrived at the south rim of the Grand Canyon on May 6, 1903. Roosevelt instantaneously realized that the Grand Canyon was "absolutely unparalleled throughout the rest of the world." Like everyone else who has stood in that place, he could not find language equal to the grandeur of the canyon. "I don't exactly know what words to use in describing it," he said. "It is beautiful and terrible and unearthly."

The president determined immediately to do whatever he could to prevent the canyon from being exploited for its mineral wealth and to prevent it from being overrun with tourist amenities.

As he looked into the abyss, Roosevelt spontaneously spoke some of the best words ever uttered about the magnificence of the American West:

I hope you will not have a building of any kind, not a summer cottage, a hotel, or anything else to mar the wonderful grandeur, the sublimity, the great loneliness and beauty of the canyon. You can not improve it. The ages have been at work on it, and man can only mar it—keep it for your children, your children's children, and for all who come after you.

After the presidential train departed for Barstow, California, Roosevelt regretted that his schedule had not permitted him more time to explore the Canyon. He also resolved to try to make the Grand Canyon a National Park after he got through the election of 1904.

Although Roosevelt was able to persuade Congress to create five new National Parks on his watch, he could not convince legislators to confer National Park status on the Grand Canyon. In the end, on January 11, 1908, he invoked the Antiquities Act (enacted by Congress in 1906) to designate Grand Canyon National Monument. Congress was adjourned at the time. At 828,000 acres, the Grand Canyon was the largest National Monument by magnitudes. The intent of the Antiquities Act was to protect historical and archaeological sites of no more than 5,000 acres. Developers and his Congressional critics howled, but increasing numbers of visitors from all over the world were so enamored of the Grand Canyon that it became politically impossible to reverse TR's executive order.

President Roosevelt surveys the "work of ages."

Roosevelt had not entirely achieved his goal, but he knew that time was now on the side of the Grand Canyon. After 1908 the canyon would never again revert to private hands. On February 29, 1919, Congress finally created Grand Canyon National Park. Unfortunately, Roosevelt did not live to see that great moment in the history of conservation. He died in his sleep on January 6, 1919, less than two months before the Congressional action.

Historian Douglas Brinkley has written, "If Roosevelt had done nothing else as president, his advocacy on behalf of preserving the canyon might well have put him in the top ranks of American presidents."

> "The ages have been at work on it, and man can only mar it."
> — THEODORE ROOSEVELT

Security was tight at Roosevelt's Washington, D.C., inaugural.

"Of course I greatly enjoyed inauguration day, and indeed I have thoroughly enjoyed being President. But I believe I can also say that I am thoroughly alive to the tremendous responsibilities of my position. Life is a long campaign where every victory merely leaves the ground free for another battle, and sooner or later defeat comes to every man, unless death forestalls it. But the final defeat does not and should not cancel the triumphs, if the latter have been substantial and for a cause worth championing."

To George Otto Trevelyan
March 9, 1905

# ROOSEVELT'S PRESIDENTIAL INAUGURATION

Theodore Roosevelt came into the presidency through the back door. President William McKinley was shot by an anarchist on September 6, 1901, in Buffalo, New York, and died on September 13. The next day, September 14, Roosevelt became the 26th president of the United States. "It's a dreadful thing to come into the Presidency in this way," he wrote, "but it would be a far worse thing to be morbid about it."

Still, Roosevelt did not wish to be remembered as an asterisk in American history.

Although it was not considered acceptable for a president to campaign openly for re-election, as the election of 1904 approached, Roosevelt did everything he could to let the American people know he would be "dee-lighted" to be re-elected. He won the 1904 election by the second largest majority up to that point in the Electoral College (336–140). It was a resounding vote of national confidence.

On the eve of his inauguration, TR wrote to John Hay, "Tomorrow I shall come into my office in my own right. Then watch out for me!" No doubt Hay, friend to TR's father and a long-suffering U.S. secretary of state, sighed at this vow of even greater strenuosity and impulsiveness from the hyper-kinetic Roosevelt. Still, Hay admired young Roosevelt. On the eve of the inauguration, he gave the president a ring containing a strand of Abraham Lincoln's hair. Roosevelt was thrilled—and profoundly moved.

> **" Tomorrow I shall come into my office in my own right. Then watch out for me! "**
> — THEODORE ROOSEVELT

Roosevelt's inaugural parade lasted three full hours on March 4, 1905, a cold day in Washington, D.C. In the procession were Rough Riders, Filipino scouts, Civil War veterans, cowboys, African Americans of the Republican Party, the Toledo Newsboys' Band, friends and neighbors from Oyster Bay, Apache chief Geronimo and Nez Perce leader Chief Joseph. Altogether 35,000 well-wishers streamed past the beaming president. TR's critics said it resembled a Roman Triumph more than a presidential inauguration.

The oath of office was administered by the Chief Justice of the Supreme Court Melville Fuller. Roosevelt placed his hand on the same Bible he had used when sworn in as New York governor, open to James 1:22-23.

Roosevelt takes the oath of office, March 4, 1905.

It was the first time telephone lines were installed at the Capitol for a presidential inauguration.

To almost everyone's astonishment, Roosevelt's inaugural address was brief—at 983 words, the fourth shortest in American history. The president suppressed the "bullys," "by Godfreys," and the wild rhetoric of his stump speeches and addressed the large crowd in rather somber terms. He ended the address with an invocation of his favorite president, Abraham Lincoln.

We in our turn have an assured confidence that we shall be able to leave this heritage unwasted and enlarged to our children and our children's children. To do so we must show, not merely in great crises, but in the everyday affairs of life, the qualities of practical intelligence, of courage, of hardihood, and endurance, and above all the power of devotion to a lofty ideal, which made great the men who founded this Republic in the days of Washington, which made great the men who preserved this Republic in the days of Abraham Lincoln.

Roosevelt spoke as if he were biting off each word.

"I am stunned by the overwhelming victory we have won. I had no conception that such a thing was possible. I thought it probable we should win, but was quite prepared to be defeated, and of course had not the slightest idea that there was such a tidal wave... The only States that went against me were those in which no free discussion is allowed and in which fraud and violence have rendered the voting a farce. I have the greatest popular majority and the greatest electoral majority ever given to a candidate for President."

To Kermit Roosevelt
November 10, 1904

# THEODORE ROOSEVELT'S RASH VOW

After filling in for assassinated President William McKinley for three years, 171 days, Theodore Roosevelt was elected in his own right on November 8, 1904.

There were no term limits in those days. Although no president had been elected to a third term in the 125-year history of the republic, Roosevelt was eligible to serve as president as many times as he could convince the American public to return him to office. Certainly few or none would have blamed him for seeking a second full term in 1908.

On election night 1904, Roosevelt stunned those around him when he impulsively announced, "The wise custom which limits the President to two terms regards the substance and not the form. Under no circumstances will I be a candidate for or accept another nomination."

Say, what? Theodore Roosevelt was the youngest president in American history, a few weeks short of 43-years-old at the time of McKinley's assassination. In 1909 he would be just 50, by any measure a man at the height of his powers. Everyone knew that Roosevelt was a political animal, a deeply ambitious man, a reformer with a legislative agenda as tall as one of the new skyscrapers gracing Manhattan Island. Why would a man so comfortable in authority renounce supreme power voluntarily?

Roosevelt had hinted to his closest political friends that he might not seek a third term, but none of them expected him to declare his intentions so soon. Henry Cabot Lodge wrote, "It had not occurred to me that you would say it at that precise moment." This was a friend's gentle rebuke to a man of power and ambition who was suddenly a lame duck. Even Roosevelt's wife Edith had been kept in the dark, almost certainly because she would have tried to talk him out of it.

In spite of the almost unbearable temptation to run again in 1908, Roosevelt kept his vow and left the presidency voluntarily on March 4, 1909. On that day, his close friend and handpicked successor William Howard Taft became the 27th president of the United States.

TR was asked many times thereafter whether he regretted the vow he had made on the night of his greatest political triumph. "Only once," he replied, "every day for the rest of my life!"

> **I would cut my hand off right here if I could recall that written statement.**
> — THEODORE ROOSEVELT TO HERMAN KOHLSAAT

Renunciation of power is a wondrous thing.

"I would cut my hand off right here," he told his friend Herman Kohlsaat, "if I could recall that written statement."

Edith and Roosevelt's closest friends were right. He should not have spoken so rashly on election night. TR was not ready to relinquish power at age 50. In fact, he spent much of the rest of his life trying to get back into the White House, beginning with his disappointing Bull Moose (Progressive) campaign of 1912. Roosevelt was a nuisance and a distraction as a former president. He could never just retire to a life of writing, hunting, and adventure.

Roosevelt's post-presidential antics led the satirist H.L. Mencken to quip that the best thing we could do with former presidents—for them and for the republic—is take them out and shoot them.

The President of the United States in repose at Yosemite.

"Lying out at night [in Yosemite] under those giant Sequoias was like lying in a temple built by no hand of man, a temple grander than any human architect could by any possibility build, and I hope for the preservation of the groves of giant trees simply because it would be a shame to our civilization to let them disappear. They are monuments in themselves. . . . In California I am impressed by how great your state is, but I am even more impressed by the immensely greater greatness that lies in the future, and I ask that your marvelous natural resources be handed on unimpaired to your posterity. We are not building this country of ours for a day. It is to last through the ages."

Address to the people of Sacramento
May 1903

# ROOSEVELT AND THE NATIONAL PARKS

Boating on Crater Lake Ore.

Early visitors repose in the serenity of Crater Lake.

Contrary to popular belief, Theodore Roosevelt did not create America's National Parks. He did play a critical role in the expansion, the definition, and the protection of the National Parks, and in the creation of the National Park System, but his work came a full generation after Yellowstone became the world's first National Park in 1872.

When Roosevelt assumed the presidency of the United States on September 14, 1901, America had five National Parks: Yellowstone (1872), Yosemite (1890), Sequoia (1890), General Grant (1890, now King's Canyon National Park), and Mount Rainier (1899). Roosevelt doubled that number to ten, and would have added the Grand Canyon, among other sites, to the National Park System, had Congress been more cooperative.

The first of Roosevelt's National Parks was Crater Lake, located in southern Oregon, established May 22, 1902. At 1,949 feet deep, Crater Lake is the deepest lake in the United States, the second deepest in North America, and the ninth deepest on earth. A man named William Gladstone Steele devoted his life to establishing and maintaining the park, which encompasses the caldera of an extinct volcano. The first Europeans to visit it were prospectors. They called it Deep Blue Lake. The earliest settlers preferred the name Crater Lake.

Roosevelt's second National Park was Wind Cave in South Dakota. It was dedicated in 1903. Approximately 95% of the world's calcite boxwork formations are found in Wind Cave. It is now considered the fourth longest cave in the world. The first recorded discovery of the cave came in 1881, just two years before Roosevelt made his buffalo-hunting trip to the Dakota badlands.

Mesa Verde became a National Park in 1906. Located in southwestern Colorado, Mesa Verde was the home of

—

" There can be no greater issue than that of conservation in this country. "

— THEODORE ROOSEVELT

—

Anasazi cliff dwellers. It wasn't until the second half of the nineteenth century that the fame of the Mesa Verde ruins reached a broad public, owing to the explorations of the local ranchers and the archaeological work of Gustaf Nordenskiöld.

Two of Roosevelt's National Parks have since been demoted.

Platt National Park was established in Oklahoma on June 29, 1906, after previously being designated (1902) as Sulphur Springs Reservation. The park area consists of partially wooded hills, springs, lakes, and streams—all improbably located in the heart of the southern Great Plains. It is now part of the Chickasaw National Recreation Area.

North Dakota's first National Park, Sullys Hill, near Devils Lake, was established in 1904. Sullys Hill, named for

General Alfred Sully, who came to Dakota Territory to chastise the Dakota Indians in the aftermath of the 1862 Minnesota Uprising, consists of marshes and wooded hills. It is now the home of buffalo, elk, and a prairie dog town. On March 3, 1931, the park was transferred to the U.S. Fish and Wildlife Service. It is now a National Game Preserve.

From 1931 to 1947 North Dakota had no National Park. On April 25, 1947, Congress established Theodore Roosevelt National Memorial Park.

Roosevelt's impact on the National Park System goes far beyond the five parks he managed to get established on his watch. With his presidential visits to Yosemite and Yellowstone (1903), his extensive writings about conservation topics, his designation of National Forests in the regions surrounding existing National Parks, his use of the National Monuments as stepping stones to later full National Park status, and his creation of the Boone and Crockett Club (1887), Roosevelt did more to promote and protect the National Park idea than almost any figure in American history.

So far as we know, Roosevelt never visited any of the National Parks he designated.

Roosevelt opposed nature gimmicks like this one at Wawona in Yosemite.

"Now there is a considerable body of public opinion in favor of keeping for our children's children, as a priceless heritage, all the delicate beauty of the lesser and all the burly majesty of the mightier forms of wild life. We are fast learning that trees must not be cut down more rapidly than they are replaced; we have taken forward steps in learning that wild beasts and birds are by right not the property merely of the people alive to-day, but the property of the unborn generations, whose belongings we have no right to squander; and there are even faint signs of our growing to understand that wild flowers should be enjoyed unplucked where they grow, and that it is barbarism to ravage the woods and fields, rooting out the mayflower and breaking branches of dogwood as ornaments for automobiles filled with jovial but ignorant picnickers from cities."

*The Outlook*
January 20, 1915

# ROOSEVELT AND THE NATIONAL MONUMENTS

Theodore Roosevelt signed the Antiquities Act on June 6, 1906. It enabled the president to designate "historic landmarks, historic and prehistoric structures, and other objects of historic or scientific interest." It was a stunning example of the legislative branch giving the president unilateral power to set aside public lands of unique archaeological or historical value *without consulting Congress.*

Historian Douglas Brinkley has written, "The Antiquities Act was to Roosevelt a contraption with which he could dictate land policy in the West, circumventing Congress."

Roosevelt made full use of this power—and as usual, strained that authority to the breaking point. His political style was always to define his authority in the broadest possible way—and then some. He regarded the Constitution and congressional legislation as enabling rather than restraining documents. It was not power per se that he sought; it was the power to accomplish mighty things.

The spirit of the legislation was that sites would be relatively small, like Devils Tower, Wyoming, which then consisted only of 1,153 acres. Congress also intended mostly to protect American Indian sites and cultural artifacts. Roosevelt stretched the legislation's term "scientific interest" to cover geology (broadly defined), which was not precisely what Congress had in mind.

Devils Tower was America's first National Monument, established on September 24, 1906, just three months after the Antiquities Act was passed. Devils Tower exemplifies the spirit of the legislation. It is unique, too magnificent to be permitted to pass into private hands, and perhaps not quite big enough in scale and variety to merit National Park status.

> " The resourceful Roosevelt had given America a way station for these places. "
> — DOUGLAS BRINKLEY

In the three years remaining in his tenure as president, Roosevelt named the first 18 National Monuments. He used the act to give permanent federal protection to such American wonders as Muir Woods just north of San Francisco (1908), Chaco Canyon, New Mexico (1907), Jewel Cave, South Dakota (1908), and Arizona's Petrified Forest (1906).

The largest of TR's National Monuments was Grand Canyon National Monument, established January 11, 1908. Roosevelt believed the Grand Canyon, which he viewed for the first time on May 6, 1903, should be made

Devils Tower was America's first National Monument.

a National Park by Congress. Congress was not about to show that kind of far-sightedness, so Roosevelt scrounged for ways to protect it from mining and adverse economic activity. Roosevelt claimed—somewhat disingenuously—that the Grand Canyon should be preserved for its prehistoric ruins. That was not his main reason for declaring the National Monument, of course, and such ruins in the canyon are comparatively meager.

Douglas Brinkley commented, "The resourceful Roosevelt had given America a way station for these places on the road to national park status."

Five of Roosevelt's National Monuments eventually graduated into National Park status: Grand Canyon (1919), Petrified Forest, Arizona (1962), Cinder Cone and Lassen Peak (now Lassen Volcanic National Park), California (1916), and Mount Olympus, Washington (now part of Olympic National Park).

Today there are 100 National Monuments in the United States. Fifteen subsequent presidents named National Monuments. Only one president has nominated as many monuments as Roosevelt: President William Clinton named 19 new monuments from 1993-2001.

Roosevelt boards the presidential yacht *Mayflower* in 1906.

"We must ever bear in mind that the great end in view is righteousness, justice as between man and man, nation and nation, the chance to lead our lives on a somewhat higher level, with a broader spirit of brotherly goodwill one for another. Peace is generally good in itself, but it is never the highest good unless it comes as the handmaid of righteousness; and it becomes a very evil thing if it serves merely as a mask for cowardice and sloth, or as an instrument to further the ends of despotism or anarchy. We despise and abhor the bully, the brawler, the oppressor, whether in private or public life, but we despise no less the coward and the voluptuary. No man is worth calling a man who will not fight rather than submit to infamy or see those that are dear to him suffer wrong. No nation deserves to exist if it permits itself to lose the stern and virile virtues; and this without regard to whether the loss is due to the growth of a heartless and all-absorbing commercialism, to prolonged indulgence in luxury and soft, effortless ease, or to the deification of a warped and twisted sentimentality."

Nobel Prize Lecture
Oslo, May 5, 1910

# ROOSEVELT AND THE NOBEL PRIZE FOR PEACE

Theodore Roosevelt was the first American to win the Nobel Peace Prize.

The Russo-Japanese War (1904-05) was a geopolitical conflict between Russia and Japan over Manchuria and Korea. Both nations had imperial designs in East Asia. Japan scored a tremendous victory over Russia at the prolonged Battle of Port Arthur in 1904. Russia, though badly defeated, refused to negotiate, hoping that the arrival of its Baltic fleet would turn the tide. Then, in the battle of Tsushima Strait, Japan annihilated the Russian navy.

The whole world was shocked.

Suddenly-industrialized Asians had defeated a white European power. Roosevelt, who always admired the Japanese, wrote, "No other nation in history has ever so quickly entered the circle of civilized powers."

Still, Roosevelt feared that if Japan pressed its military advantage to its logical conclusion, Russia would be so severely defeated and humiliated that it would upset the balance of power in Asia. He was frankly glad that the plucky Japanese had defeated the haughty Russians, but he knew too that imperial hubris might lead them to challenge America's growing interests in the Pacific, including Hawaii.

In 1905, Roosevelt invited representatives of Japan and Russia to come to the United States to negotiate a peace. Roosevelt intervened in the war without consulting Congress, the State Department, or even his cabinet. The great European powers scoffed that upstart America would presume to wade into diplomatic waters better left to seasoned professionals.

It would be the last time Europe underestimated the ambition, strength, and confidence of the American people.

> *Peace is generally good in itself, but it is never the highest good unless it comes as the handmaid of righteousness.*
>
> — THEODORE ROOSEVELT

Representatives of the belligerents met with Roosevelt informally at Sagamore Hill, his New York home, during the summer of 1905. They came on separate occasions, and their experiences could not have been more different. Russian Count Sergei Witte, visiting on August 4, 1905, was appalled by the lack of formal protocol at the president's home. He found luncheon at Sagamore "almost indigestible," and was miffed that the food had been served without wine or even a tablecloth. Japan's Baron Jutaro Komura was charmed by the informal democratic manners of Roosevelt. He remembered that when it came time for bed, the president personally led him upstairs while holding a candle.

By August 18, formal peace negotiations in Portsmouth, New Hampshire, had broken down. Roosevelt telegraphed the Japanese emperor and Russia's Czar

President Roosevelt with representatives of Russia and Japan.

Nicholas II. He reminded the czar that the Japanese had destroyed the Russian navy and that Japan was not asking for any land on the Russian mainland. He reminded the Japanese emperor that Japan had gained a stunning victory that could hardly be improved upon by more loss of blood and money.

Eventually, the Japanese settled for the southern half of Sakhalin Island, and agreed—with extreme reluctance—to give up demands for a financial indemnity.

Roosevelt won the Nobel Peace Prize in 1906—the first American to win in any category. He collected his prize in Christiana, Norway, on May 5, 1910, after his yearlong safari in Africa. It would have been simply impossible for the former president to extol peace without providing characteristically Rooseveltian statements about realism in world affairs:

No man is worth calling a man who will not fight rather than submit to infamy or see those that are dear to him suffer wrong. No nation deserves to exist if it permits itself to lose the stern and virile virtues."

Roosevelt donated the prize money to charity.

Upton Sinclair at the height of his fame.

"Because of things I have done on behalf of justice to the workingman, I have often been called a Socialist. Usually I have not taken the trouble even to notice the epithet. I am not afraid of names, and I am not one of those who fear to do what is right because someone else will confound me with partisans with whose principles I am not in accord. Moreover, I know that many American Socialists are high-minded and honorable citizens, who in reality are merely radical social reformers. They are oppressed by the brutalities and industrial injustices which we see everywhere about us. When I recall how often I have seen Socialists and ardent non-Socialists working side by side for some specific measure of social or industrial reform, and how I have found opposed to them on the side of privilege many shrill reactionaries who insist on calling all reformers Socialists, I refuse to be panic-stricken by having this title mistakenly applied to me."

*Autobiography*

# ROOSEVELT AND UPTON SINCLAIR

In 1906 socialist writer Upton Sinclair published his exposé of the meat packing industry, *The Jungle*. The book was serialized in several national journals. The socialist journal *One Hoss Philosophy* published long extracts, although the editors chose not to print an episode in which a female meat packer gives birth to her baby on the job, and the baby winds up being made into sausage!

The sanctity of the nation's food supply had become a serious issue by the beginning of the twentieth century. When the nation had consisted mostly of self-sufficient farmers, everyone had been responsible for their own food supply. But with the coming of the age of industry and the heavy concentration of population in the nation's great cities, millions of people got their meat from industrial suppliers, and they had no way of insuring that the food they purchased was safe.

Sinclair's publisher had sagely timed the release of *The Jungle* to coincide with the U.S. Senate's debate on the Pure Food and Drug Act. Of his book, Sinclair said, "I aimed at the public's heart, and by accident I hit it in the stomach."

President Roosevelt read *The Jungle*. He was sickened by the conditions Sinclair described, though he assumed the novelist had exaggerated them for sensational effect. At the same time, Roosevelt was indignant over Sinclair's attempts to use the book to promote socialism. He wrote a querulous but respectful letter to the author on March 15, 1906. Roosevelt gave Sinclair a lecture on the virtues of capitalism and its capacity to clean up its abuses under government supervision, but at the end of the letter he returned to the specifics of the meat packing industry: "But all this has nothing to do with the fact that the specific evils you point out shall, if their existence be proved, and if I have power, be eradicated."

> **❝ I aimed at the public's heart, and by accident I hit it in the stomach. ❞**
>
> — UPTON SINCLAIR

Roosevelt summoned Sinclair to Washington, D.C., to meet with him personally and to participate in conferences about the reform of the meat packing industry. Sinclair was as surprised as he was flattered. "A President of the United States," he later wrote, "talking in the presence of a wholly irresponsible and desperately determined young Socialist agitator, ought to exercise at least a little reserve and caution. But apparently that point of view had not occurred to Teddy." In other words, Sinclair was surprised by how completely the president had accepted his allegations.

Otto von Bismarck said, "He who likes sausage or law should never watch the making of either."

Meanwhile, in the *Saturday Evening Post*, meat mogul J. Ogden Armour promised the American people that Sinclair's allegations were untrue: "In Armour & Co.'s business not one atom of any condemned animal or carcass finds its way, directly or indirectly, from any source, into any food product or food ingredient." This patently false claim so enraged President Roosevelt that he threatened to release the results of the government's independent investigation of the meat packing industry, the Neill-Reynolds Meat Inspection Report.

Public outrage—as well as public demand for a clean and safe meat industry—led to the passage of landmark federal legislation. The Pure Food and Drug Act of 1906 forbade the manufacture, sale, or transportation of adulterated or fraudulently labeled food and drugs in the United States. The Meat Inspection Act mandated federal inspection of all slaughterhouses engaged in interstate commerce, and enforced sanitary regulation of the industry.

The Socialist agitator and author, coupled with our readingest president, had influenced the course of American history.

Quentin Roosevelt and an unnamed friend plotting mischief.

"You colored men and women must set your faces like flint against those who would preach to you the gospel of envy, hatred, and bitterness. May you realize that the way in which you can help your fellow citizens as well as the members of your race, is not by empty declarations, least of all by preaching vindictiveness and hatred, but by leading your lives as every-day citizens in such fashion that they shall add to the sum total of good citizenship. When you succeed in getting the ordinary white man of the community to realize that the ordinary colored man is a good citizen you have a friend in him, and that white man is benefited so greatly that there is only one person who receives a greater benefit, and that is the colored man himself."

Address to the National Negro Business League
August 19, 1910

# ROOSEVELT AND AFRICAN AMERICANS

Theodore Roosevelt's record on race is decidedly mixed. He famously invited Booker T. Washington to dine with him in the White House, the first African American to be served rather than serve in that famous house. When a storm of political protest ensued, Roosevelt was defiant—but he never invited another African American to dinner during his two terms as president.

In Cuba, on July 1, 1898, Roosevelt's Rough Riders fought beside black soldiers of the Ninth and Tenth Cavalry. Roosevelt justly praised the black troops, but he also noted in his book *The Rough Riders,* "Under the strain the colored infantrymen began to get a little uneasy and drift to the rear...This I could not allow."

In August 1906, African American infantrymen from Fort Brown were accused of shooting up the town of Brownsville, Texas, killing one white citizen and wounding another. We now know that the black troops were innocent. Because the black troops refused to cooperate with the investigation, however, President Roosevelt discharged without honor the entire regiment of 167 soldiers, but not their white officers. Six of the soldiers had earned the Medal of Freedom for their actions in Cuba or the Philippines.

> *" Murder is murder,*
> *whether black or white. "*
> — THEODORE ROOSEVELT

It soon became clear that President Roosevelt had over-reacted and condemned the innocent without solid evidence. Roosevelt stubbornly refused to reconsider the case. Although he was a lifelong believer in the rights of individual African Americans, he never came to terms with African Americans as a social group. Roosevelt was notoriously antagonistic to "hyphenated Americans," no matter what their racial, ethnic, or national origins. Many African Americans, who had come to see Roosevelt as their champion, permanently lost respect for him after the Brownsville incident.

**Footnote:** The 167 soldiers were finally cleared after publication of John Weaver's 1970 book, *The Brownsville Incident.*

The tables turned in summer of 1917 when race riots broke out in a number of American cities. In St. Louis, at least 39 African Americans were killed in what has been called the worst labor-related riot in American history. In New York that summer, Roosevelt attended a gathering honoring Russia's new Kerensky government. He took the opportunity to denounce the riots. This led the great

Tea pickers sing folk songs for President Roosevelt in Summerville, South Carolina.

labor leader Samuel Gompers, at the same podium, to publicly defend the white rioters, saying they were merely fighting to protect their jobs in the wake of waves of black immigration from the rural south to urban centers.

Theodore Roosevelt became so enraged by Gompers' rationalization for race prejudice that he rushed across the stage and shook his fist in Gomper's face. "Murder is murder, whether black or white," he shouted.

He called for a federal investigation of the riot. "I am not willing that a meeting called to commemorate the birth of democracy in Russia shall even seem to have expressed or to have accepted apologies for the brutal infamies imposed on colored people...Let there be the fullest investigation into these murders."

This spontaneous outburst did a good deal to heal his relations with the African American community.

These incidents do not represent the sum total of Roosevelt's actions concerning African Americans, but they give a sense of the complexity of his race relations in and out of office.

Harvard and Princeton face off, 1913.

"It is to my mind simple nonsense, a mere confession of weakness, to desire to abolish a game because tendencies show themselves, or practices grow up, which prove that the game ought to be reformed. Take football, for instance. The preparatory schools are able to keep football clean and to develop the right spirit in the players without the slightest necessity ever arising to so much as consider the question of abolishing it. …If necessary, let the college authorities interfere to stop any excess or perversion, making their interference as little officious as possible, and yet as rigorous as is necessary to achieve the end. But there is no justification for stopping a thoroughly manly sport because it is sometimes abused, when the experience of every good preparatory school shows that the abuse is in no shape necessarily attendant upon the game."

Address at the Harvard Union
February 23, 1907

# ROOSEVELT SAVES COLLEGE FOOTBALL

Theodore Roosevelt faced many important issues during the course of his presidency, from the Russo-Japanese War to the digging of the Panama Canal. Although he did not live through so critical a time in American history as his hero Abraham Lincoln or his fifth cousin Franklin Roosevelt, he served as president during the dramatic first years of the twentieth century. He led America, sometimes kicking and screaming, into the modern age. For all of that, he found time to pay attention to things that might seem beneath presidential notice.

At the beginning of his second term, for example, President Roosevelt helped to save college football.

In 1905 alone, 18 young men had died from injuries sustained while playing football. Gang tackling was the rule, and an offensive formation called the flying wedge literally mowed over the opposition. Players wore minimal headgear and padding. American football was then a great deal closer to rugby than it was to the modern game.

Together with the administrations of other elite universities, Harvard President Charles Elliott threatened to abolish football if its violence and injury rate could not be diminished. The death of a young man named Harold Moore in the Union-N.Y.U. game in 1905 had brought national attention to the brutality of the sport. *McClure's Magazine* published an exposé which argued that college football violated the ideal of amateur sportsmanship and fair play.

Roosevelt did not much like Elliott, who was among other things an anti-imperialist. TR did not want Elliott to abolish or "emasculate football."

The Harvard Football team takes the field, ca. 1910.

On October 9, 1905, Roosevelt summoned representatives from the Big Three (Harvard, Princeton, and Yale) to the White House. His goal was to find a way to minimize the danger of injury in football without putting the game "on too ladylike a basis." Roosevelt didn't mind hard hitting so long as it was done "on a thoroughly clean basis."

> " In life, as in a football game, the principle to follow is: Hit the line hard; don't foul and don't shirk, but hit the line hard! "
>
> — THEODORE ROOSEVELT

In December 1905, Chancellor Henry M. MacCracken of New York University convened a meeting of 13 colleges and universities to initiate changes in football rules. As a result, the American Football Rules Committee was created. In 1906, a new set of gridiron rules was adopted. Referees were added to police the activity on the playing field. A neutral zone was created at the line of scrimmage.

The ten-yard first down rule was adopted. Mass formations and gang tackling were banned. The forward pass was introduced.

All of this president-inspired emergency activity changed the nature of college football and led to the creation of the National College Athletic Association. On December 28, 1905, the Intercollegiate Athletic Association of the United States (IAAUS) was founded with 62 charter members. In 1910 it assumed its present name, the NCAA.

In 1907 the *Independent* lauded TR's efforts to reform college football: "We are glad to bear witness that football as now played under the new rules is far more interesting to the spectator than formerly."

Roosevelt's attempts to reform collegiate football had nothing to do with the plight of his eldest son, Ted, who went out for football during his freshman year at Harvard and had a rough time of it. Opposing teams piled on him and purposely broke Ted's nose. The president regarded this as routine "life in the arena."

Roosevelt in the pages of *Puck*, contemplates English orthography.

"It is not an attack on the language of Shakespeare and Milton, because it is in some instances a going back to the forms they used, and in others merely the extension of changes which, as regards other words, have taken place since their time.

It is not an attempt to do anything far-reaching or sudden or violent; or indeed anything very great at all. It is merely an attempt to cast what slight weight can properly be cast on the side of the popular forces which are endeavoring to make our spelling a little less foolish and fantastic."

To Charles A. Stillings
Public Printer of the United States
August 27, 1906

# THEODORE ROOSEVELT AND SPELLING REFORM

During his second term as president, Theodore Roosevelt undertook a quixotic campaign to simplify American spelling.

The history of the English language is replete with failed attempts to reform spelling, dating back to the Renaissance.

Roosevelt had become a convert to a spelling reform movement that emanated from Columbia University, where he had briefly studied law. Somehow the proposals of the "Simplified Spelling Board" captured the president's fancy. Edith quipped that it was because her husband was such a poor speller "and wished a wide latitude in consequence." Roosevelt's friends and Spelling Board founders Thomas Lounsbury and Brander Matthews had been advocating orthographic reform for years, with the help of grants from Andrew Carnegie.

Roosevelt was a cultural nationalist. He wanted the United States to achieve cultural independence from Great Britain, to cherish our own characteristic national speech and not to continue expressing our unique national experience through the filter of British English. The president believed that spelling reform would help differentiate the use of English on opposite shores of the Atlantic Ocean.

On August 23, 1906, without consulting Congress, President Roosevelt issued an executive order directing the Government Printing Office to adopt a list of 300 reformed spellings recommended by the Simplified Spelling Board. He directed that his Annual Message to Congress in 1906 be printed in simplified English.

The Spelling Board idealists wisely sought to eliminate the letter "u" from such words as honor and labor. But the reform list also included such new spellings as "addresst," "blusht," "kist," "partizan," "phenix," "thru," "winkt," and "comprize." This proved to be too much for the American people and their elected representatives.

To say that Congress balked is an understatement. President Roosevelt was savagely criticized for meddling with the mother tongue in a high-handed and unconstitutional way. He was mocked for extending his presidential authority into minutiae. Congressman Champ Clark of Mississippi publicly asked when the United States might elect a president "who will attend strictly to his constitutional functions and expend his energies only on subjects of great pith and moment."

Congress actually passed a stern joint resolution refusing to accept Roosevelt's reforms for official documents of the United States government. The Supreme Court declared that it would simply ignore the presidential edict. The major

> *"THIS IZ TU MUTCH."*
>
> — HARPER'S WEEKLY

Equal opportunity strenuosity: from the Russo-Japanese War to spelling reform.

newspapers of America were openly derisive. The *New York Times*, for example, declared it would regard any reformed spellings issued by the federal government as misspellings and correct them before publication.

*Harper's Weekly* proclaimed, "THIS IZ TU MUTCH." The *Baltimore Sun* asked if TR would now spell his name "Rusevelt" or "Butt-in-sky."

In derision, Roosevelt's critics began to say that in America it was not the King's English, but "the President's English."

Roosevelt wistfully rescinded his executive order while declaring defiantly that he would continue to employ Simplified Spelling in his correspondence. (He did not.) Of his 300 reformist spellings, he wrote, a little sadly, "If they do not ultimately meet with popular approval they will be dropt, and that is all there is about it."

Thereafter, Roosevelt blusht and kist his wif and addresst the nation in the old time-worn way.

TR and Edith at a Naval Review off Long Island, 1903.

"In my own judgment the most important service that I rendered to peace was the voyage of the battle fleet round the world. I had become convinced that for many reasons it was essential that we should have it clearly understood, by our own people especially, but also by other peoples, that the Pacific was as much our home waters as the Atlantic, and that our fleet could and would at will pass from one to the other of the two great oceans. It seemed to me evident that such a voyage would greatly benefit the navy itself; would arouse popular interest in and enthusiasm for the navy; and would make foreign nations accept as a matter of course that our fleet should from time to time be gathered in the Pacific, just as from time to time it was gathered in the Atlantic, and that its presence in one ocean was no more to be accepted as a mark of hostility to any Asiatic power than its presence in the Atlantic was to be accepted as a mark of hostility to any European power."

*Autobiography*

# ROOSEVELT AND THE GREAT WHITE FLEET

Theodore Roosevelt was a huge advocate of a strong U.S. Navy. His first major book was *The Naval War of 1812,* begun when he was a senior at Harvard and published in 1882. After reading Alfred Thayer Mahan's *The Influence of Sea Power on History* (1890), he determined to do everything in his power to increase the size of the U.S. Navy and convince the American people that such expenditures were essential to American security and success in the world arena.

Between 1897-98, Roosevelt served as the assistant secretary of the Navy in the administration of William McKinley. Roosevelt pressed for war against Spain, particularly after the sinking of the *Maine* in Havana harbor on February 15, 1898. When President McKinley finally decided to take the United States to war, Roosevelt resigned from his post and formed his "harum scarum" troupe of Rough Riders.

TR's heroism in Cuba propelled him first into the governorship of New York (1898-1900), then into the vice presidency (1901), from which he ascended to the presidency upon the assassination of William McKinley in September 1901.

When Roosevelt became president, the United States had the fifth largest navy in the world. By the time he left the presidency, the U.S. could boast the second largest navy (depending a little on how you count).

Towards the end of his second term in 1907, without consulting either Congress or his cabinet, Roosevelt decided to send the entire U.S. fleet on a round-the-world cruise. America's 16 battleships and a large number of support vessels, all painted white for the

The Great White Fleet returns to America, February 22,1909.

global parade, left Hampton Roads on December 16, 1907, and returned, 43,000 nautical miles and 20 port calls on six continents later, on February 22, 1909. Roosevelt was present on both occasions, waving his hat to cheer on the ships and crying "bully," "by Godfrey," and "Isn't this a great moment for America," to anybody who would listen.

> " Isn't this a great moment for America! "
>
> — THEODORE ROOSEVELT

The audacious round-the-world cruise accomplished many things. It announced to the world in an unmistakable manner that the United States was now a great power. It demonstrated America's ability to protect its west coast (before the digging of the Panama Canal),

to dispatch its fleet anywhere in the world, to provision it and keep it supplied with coal, and to coordinate the logistics of so massive a naval maneuver. It also served as an indication of the triumph of executive power in Roosevelt's America.

An irate congressman told the president in no uncertain terms that he had broken Senate protocol in dispatching the fleet without seeking approval of Congress, that his precipitousness might touch off an international incident or even war, and that there was not enough money in the Navy budget to send the fleet completely around the world.

Roosevelt recorded his response in his *Autobiography* (1913): "I announced in response that I had enough money to take the fleet around to the Pacific anyhow, that the fleet would certainly go, and that if Congress did not choose to appropriate enough money to get the fleet back, why, it would stay in the Pacific. There was no further difficulty about the money."

Cowboy life was exhausting, dirty, and often lonely.

"When utterly tired, it was hard to have to get up for one's trick at night herd. Nevertheless, on ordinary nights the two hours round the cattle in the still darkness were pleasant. The loneliness, under the vast empty sky, and the silence in which the breathing of the cattle sounded loud, and the alert readiness to meet any emergency which might suddenly arise out of the formless night, all combined to give one a sense of subdued interest... The punchers on night guard usually rode round the cattle in reverse directions; calling and singing to them if the beasts seemed restless, to keep them quiet."

*Autobiography*

# ROOSEVELT AND THE MUSIC OF THE AMERICAN WEST

Theodore Roosevelt had the capacity to be completely present wherever he went. Although he was a man of aristocratic birth and education, he liked to mingle with average Americans—to work alongside them, to listen to their speech, and to try to discover the core of the American character.

During badlands cattle roundups, Roosevelt threw himself into every variety of work. His principle was to do whatever was required, no matter how exhausting, dirty, or difficult. The future president wanted to soak up every possible frontier experience, before it was too late. Historian Hermann Hagedorn wrote, "He plunged into the life of the Bad Lands seeking to comprehend the emotions and the mental processes, the personalities and the social conditions that made it what it was."

On one unfortunate occasion, Roosevelt was attempting to direct some errant calves back to the herd. Without thinking, he blurted out to one of his men, "Hasten forward quickly there!" There was, says Hagedorn, "a roar of delight from the cowpunchers, and instantly, the phrase became a part of the vocabulary of the Bad Lands." Cowboys began to use the phrase in a variety of situations. There was even a drink in a Medora saloon called the "Hasten Forward," in honor of the colorful easterner.

At some point Roosevelt realized the talk and music of Dakota Territory represented an authentic American folk culture that would fade away once the frontier era ended. He believed frontier culture should be recorded so that

♪ I see by your outfit that you are a cowboy. ♪

the extraordinary era would linger in American memory. He was particularly fascinated by frontier ballads that were almost invariably adaptations of existing songs from the Anglo-Gaelic tradition.

> ## " Hasten forward quickly there! "
>
> — THEODORE ROOSEVELT

In his *Autobiography* (1913) Roosevelt wrote, "The punchers on night guard usually rode round the cattle in reverse directions; calling and singing to them if the beasts seemed restless, to keep them quiet." The root of the cowboy music tradition is embedded in this great sentence.

Roosevelt encouraged his friend Owen Wister to write novels that captured the spirit of the frontier. Wister dedicated *The Virginian* (1902) to Roosevelt and set one scene in the novel in Medora. Roosevelt also encouraged the work of badlands cowboy poet laureate James Foley.

Roosevelt entreated Texas musicologist and folklorist John Lomax to record the songs and poems of the American West before it was too late. Lomax's book, *Cowboy Songs and Other Frontier Ballads* (1910), is an American classic. Roosevelt wrote the preface:

Under modern conditions . . . the native ballad is speedily killed by competition with the music hall songs; the cowboys becoming ashamed to sing the crude homespun ballads in view of what Owen Wister calls the 'ill-smelling saloon cleverness' of the far less interesting compositions of the music-hall singers. It is therefore a work of real importance to preserve permanently this unwritten ballad literature of the back country and the frontier.

Roosevelt was not merely a conservationist with respect to natural resources. He was equally determined to conserve the authentic frontier culture he had shared and personally helped to shape.

In 1901, one of Roosevelt's detractors said, with grudging admiration, "That damned cowboy has become the president of the United States."

TR was unrelenting in a fight.

"It happens that in the matter of drinking I am an extremely abstemious man; I suppose that no man not a total abstainer could well drink less than I do; and whiskey and brandy I practically never touch. The accusation that I ever have been addicted in the slightest degree to drinking to excess, or to drinking even wine—and liquor, as I say, I practically never touch—in any but the most moderate way, is not only the blackest falsehood; it does not represent any distortion or exaggeration; it has not slightest basis in fact; it is simply malignant invention—just as sheer an invention as if they had said that at the age of five I had poisoned my grandmother or had been mixed up in the assassination of Lincoln by Wilkes Booth. One accusation would be exactly as infamous and exactly as ludicrous as the other."

Letter of February 25, 1909

# ROOSEVELT AND THE LIBEL SUIT

On October 12, 1912, towards the end of the Bull Moose presidential campaign, the Ishpeming, Michigan, *Iron Ore* published the following statement: "Roosevelt lies and curses in a most disgusting way; he gets drunk too, and that not infrequently, and all his intimate friends know about it."

If editor George S. Newett had known what a tsunami of righteous indignation he would unleash with that one unfortunate sentence, he would never have printed it.

It was easy to see why Newett might regard Theodore Roosevelt as an intoxicated man. His behavior was so hectic and over-the-top at all times that it was hard to believe he was not pouring something into his gigantic cups of coffee. Even his friend Henry Adams wrote, "Theodore is never sober, only he is drunk with himself and not with rum." His election rival William Howard Taft said, "I think the intoxication was altogether with his own verbosity. I would make an excellent witness in his defense."

> "Theodore is never sober, only he is drunk with himself and not with rum."
> — HENRY ADAMS

After the Bull Moose campaign ended, Roosevelt sued Newett for libel.

The May 1913 trial was held in Marquette, Michigan. The jury consisted of four farmers, two miners, two teamsters, a clerk, a blacksmith, a locomotive fireman, and a lumberjack.

As in all of the controversies of his life, Roosevelt engaged in overkill. Seventeen of his associates

Roosevelt's relations with the press were usually "dee-lightful."

provided sworn depositions declaring him sober, and 19 more testified in person. Historian Patricia O'Toole commented, "There were three former cabinet secretaries in the courtroom, along with several distinguished journalists, two of his physicians, former Secret Service agents, and aides who had been at his side day and night."

The joke in Marquette was that you couldn't throw a brick through the courthouse window without striking someone important.

Newett withdrew his allegations and offered an apology, but Roosevelt was not done with the hapless editor.

He took the stand and gave what amounted to an autobiography of his lifetime experience with alcoholic beverages. He declared that he had never drunk "a highball or a cocktail in my life," that he never took a drop of whiskey or brandy, "except as I drink it under the direction of a doctor." Roosevelt said that although he sometimes took a glass of light wine, "I do not drink beer." Of his years in Dakota Territory, he declared, "I don't believe that I ever went into a saloon in the western

country except where it was at a little hotel, where the only two rooms would be a kitchen and a dining room."

Rising to his full righteousness, Roosevelt declared, "I have never been drunk or in the slightest degree under the influence of liquor."

The judge instructed the jury to return a verdict for the plaintiff (TR), then asked Roosevelt what sort of punitive damages he sought. Roosevelt replied, "I did not go into this suit for money. I went into it... because I wished, once and for all, during my own lifetime, to deal with these slanders, fully, and comprehensively, so that never again will it be possible for any man, in good faith, to repeat them. I have achieved my purpose, and I am content."

Accordingly, the Michigan court awarded Roosevelt the legal minimum of damages: six cents.

The trial had cost him an estimated $40,000 to litigate.

Every inch a king: TR at the height of his power, 1904.

"Surely there never was a fight better worth making than the one in which we are engaged. It little matters what befalls any one of us who for the time being stand in the forefront of the battle. I hope we shall win, and I believe that if we can wake the people to what the fight really means we shall win. But, win or lose, we shall not falter. Whatever fate may at the moment overtake any of us, the movement itself will not stop. Our cause is based on the eternal principles of righteousness; and even though we who now lead may for the time fail, in the end the cause itself shall triumph... Now to you men, who, in your turn, have come together to spend and be spent in the endless crusade against wrong, to you who face the future resolute and confident, to you who strive in a spirit of brotherhood for the betterment of our Nation, to you who gird yourselves for this great new fight in the never-ending warfare for the good of humankind, I say in closing what in that speech I said in closing: We stand at Armageddon, and we battle for the Lord."

"A Confession of Faith"
Bull Moose Convention
August 6, 1912

# ROOSEVELT AND THE BULL MOOSE CAMPAIGN

Theodore Roosevelt was elected only once to the presidency of the United States. And yet he served a total of seven years, 171 days as president, ascending to the office on September 14, 1901, after the assassination of William McKinley. He stood for election in his own right in 1904 and won resoundingly. On election night 1904, Roosevelt vowed not to stand for re-election in 1908, an impulsive move that shocked his closest supporters. He left office voluntarily on March 4, 1909, at age 50.

Roosevelt handpicked his successor, William Howard Taft, a dear friend who had been the American proconsul in the Philippines and who served as Roosevelt's second secretary of war. Taft proved to be a weak president. He veered away from some of Roosevelt's presidential initiatives, particularly on conservation. Roosevelt became so disenchanted with Taft that he decided to challenge him for the Republican nomination in 1912.

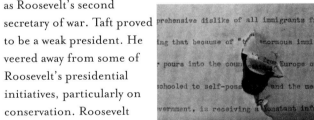

The bullet-riddled speech.

Roosevelt won most of the newfangled presidential primaries in 1912. Republican bosses still controlled the party process in that era, however, and Taft was able to secure the nomination in spite of TR's immense national popularity. Roosevelt cried foul. He was so enraged by what he regarded as a stolen nomination that he uncharacteristically bolted from the Republican Party and formed the Progressive (or Bull Moose) Party, accepted its nomination in Chicago on August 6, 1912,

Roosevelt addresses the Progressive Party Convention at Armageddon (Chicago).

and famously announced, "We stand at Armageddon and we battle for the Lord." In many respects, the Bull Moose campaign of 1912 was more of a moral crusade and a social movement than a traditional political campaign.

The Progressives called themselves the Bull Moose Party because, as always, Roosevelt professed that he felt "fit as a bull moose."

The Bull Moose Party sought to abolish child labor and the seven-day work week, provide financial aid to workers injured on the job, create a broad program of social insurance for those unable to work, and mandate a living wage. It advocated women's suffrage, federal management of public health, and the creation of a government body to improve conditions of rural life. The party called for tariff reforms and a commission to regulate large industrial corporations.

Just three weeks before the election, Roosevelt survived an assassination attempt. He was in Milwaukee, Wisconsin, on October 14, 1912, on his way to give a speech, when saloon keeper John Schrank shot him in the chest at point blank range. Roosevelt delivered an 84-minute speech before seeking medical attention. "It takes more than that to kill a bull moose," he inevitably

declared. All candidates briefly suspended their campaigns. The incident did not change the outcome of the election on November 5, 1912. Roosevelt made a full recovery.

> " It takes more than that to kill a bull moose. "
>
> — THEODORE ROOSEVELT

In the end, Roosevelt lost the presidential election of 1912, though he took second and received the largest third party vote in American history (27.4%). Taft received just 23% of the vote. (He later went to become a distinguished chief justice of the U.S. Supreme Court). Democratic candidate Woodrow Wilson won the election with 41.8% of the vote. Wilson instituted many of the reforms advocated by the Bull Moose Party.

From the pages of *Puck*, the White House East Room in the Roosevelt Years.

"Our tents were pitched in a small open glade a hundred yards from the dead elephant. The night was clear, the stars shone brightly, and in the west the young moon hung just above the line of tall tree-tops. Fires were speedily kindled and the men sat around them, feasting and singing in a strange minor tone until late in the night. The flickering light left them at one moment in black obscurity, and the next brought into bold relief their sinewy crouching figures, their dark faces, gleaming eyes, and flashing teeth… I toasted slices of elephant's heart on a pronged stick before the fire, and found it delicious; for I was hungry, and the night was cold."

*African Game Trails*

# ROOSEVELT ON SAFARI

When he left the presidency in 1909, Theodore Roosevelt undertook a yearlong safari in Africa. He told his aide Archie Butt that the safari "will let me down to private life without that dull thud of which we hear so much."

Eighteen-year-old Kermit took a leave of absence from Harvard to accompany his father. Roosevelt and Kermit left Hoboken, New Jersey, on March 23, 1909, just three weeks after TR left the presidency.

Roosevelt's wife Edith later recalled, "It was a dreadful day. I have never known but one like it; that day when [son] Archie's fate was in doubt and we did not know if he would live or not." Although Edith met Roosevelt in Khartoum, Sudan, a year after his departure, she was heartbroken that he had chosen to spend the first year of his retirement away from her.

> ## "I speak of Africa and golden joys."
>
> — THEODORE ROOSEVELT

On the eve of his departure, his old antagonist J.P. Morgan quipped, "America hopes that every lion will do its duty."

The Roosevelts reached Mambosa on the East African coast on April 21, 1909. Roosevelt was so excited that he rode into the heart of Africa strapped to the cowcatcher on the front of the train. With 260 porters, their expedition was one of the largest safaris ever mounted in Africa. Roosevelt and Kermit hunted in British East Africa (today's Kenya) and the Belgian Congo.

Bwana Makuba (Great Master) with one of his eight elephants.

The natives called TR "Bwana Makuba" (Great Master). They christened Kermit as "Bwana Merodadi" (Dandy Master). Father found this more amusing than son.

Although Roosevelt wanted to hunt African game, he did not want the public to think he was making the trip to bag great quadrupeds. He convinced the Smithsonian Institution to send along three field naturalists and taxidermists. Thus he was able to call it a scientific not merely a hunting expedition. Even so, Roosevelt's old nemesis, Nelson A. Miles, declared that any man who shot elephants for pleasure "must have a depraved mind."

Roosevelt was determined not to leave Africa without bagging the five most dangerous game animals: elephant, rhinoceros, buffalo, leopard, and lion. He got nine lions, eight elephants, 13 rhinoceroses, six buffaloes, and other mammals. The expedition's scientific contribution to the Smithsonian included 8,463 vertebrates, 550 large mammals, 3,379 small mammals, and 2,784 birds.

Scribner's magazine paid TR $50,000 for a series of articles about the trip. The resulting book, African Game Trails, became a big game classic. The book begins with a magnificent passage reminiscent of epic poetry: "I speak of Africa and golden joys; the joy of wandering through lonely lands; the joy of hunting the mighty and terrible lords of the wilderness..."

As usual, Roosevelt could not undertake such a journey without carrying along books to read. His sister Corinne put together 60 titles (world classics, in several languages) trimmed to pocket size and bound in pigskin to withstand rigors of the African climate and travel. TR called it his Pigskin Library.

At the end of his adventure, Roosevelt caught up with long-suffering Edith in Khartoum. Together they undertook a three-month tour of Europe.

Roosevelt, diminished, returns from the River of Doubt.

No less than six weeks were spent slowly and with peril and exhausting labor forcing our way down through what seemed a literally endless succession of rapids and cataracts. In passing those rapids we lost five of the seven canoes with which we started and had to build others. One of our best men lost his life in the rapids. Under the strain one of the men went completely bad, shirked all his work, stole his comrades' food and when punished by the sergeant he with cold-blooded deliberation murdered the sergeant and fled into the wilderness. Colonel Rondon's dog running ahead of him while hunting, was shot by two Indians; by his death he in all probability saved the life of his master."

*Through the Brazilian Wilderness*

# ROOSEVELT AND THE RIVER OF DOUBT

After the failure of his third party (Bull Moose) bid for the presidency in 1912, Theodore Roosevelt accepted invitations to lecture on foreign policy in several South American nations.

Following the lecture tour, Roosevelt planned to make a tame trip by steamer up the Paraguay River and down rivers of the Amazon basin. Things changed dramatically when Roosevelt was invited to join Brazil's Colonel Candido Rondon (1865-1958) in exploring one of the last significant uncharted rivers in the world.

Rondon (the Lewis & Clark of Brazil) had recently discovered a river that he designated the River of Doubt because its course, length, and mouth were unknown.

Roosevelt jumped at the opportunity: "It's my last chance to be a boy."

When Henry Fairfield Osborn of the American Museum of Natural History learned of Roosevelt's change of plans, he expressed alarm. The museum, he indicated, might refuse to support the extreme adventure. Nothing could be more disastrous than to have a former president perish under its sponsorship. Roosevelt sent back a cable, bristling with defiance: "Tell Osborn I have already lived and enjoyed as much of life as any nine other men I know; I have had my full share, and if it is necessary for me to leave my bones in South America, I am quite ready to do so."

Kermit Roosevelt, 24, was working in South America. He accompanied his father on the great river journey. The expedition embarked on the River of Doubt on February 27, 1914, with a crew of 22 men. The great adventure soon turned into something of an ordeal. "We were about to go into the unknown, and no one could say what it held," said Rondon.

One crew member drowned. Another mutinied, then murdered his superior. Indians shot the expedition's dog. Several canoes were lost in accidents, along with much of their food. Dank air, fierce insects including fire ants, wasps, ticks, and mosquitoes made it nearly impossible to work or sleep. Deadly piranhas haunted the waters. A range of diseases ravaged the expedition. Eventually everyone was seriously malnourished.

A month into the journey, Roosevelt injured his left leg while attempting to pry a canoe from the rocks, the same leg injured in a carriage and tram accident in 1902. Eventually, suffering from malaria and an infection in his leg, beset with a gastrointestinal complaint, Roosevelt descended into delirium. The former president implored Kermit and Rondon to go on without him and at least save themselves. They refused.

Roosevelt and Colonel Rondon on the River of Doubt.

When the party finally reached civilization at Manaos, an ambulance carried one of the toughest of all Americans to the local hospital. Roosevelt had lost 57 pounds. In an age before antibiotics, his health was broken. He lived another five years, but never fully recovered. His friend William Roscoe Thayer later said, "The Brazilian wilderness stole ten years away of his life."

> "It's my last chance to be a boy."
>
> — THEODORE ROOSEVELT

Still, historian Stacy Cordery has written, "The journey was a spectacular success, for it resulted in the charting of a wholly unmapped river and the acquisition of over a thousand birds and mammals, some completely unknown to Western science at the time."

Peaceful Valley Ranch — Medora, N.D.

Roosevelt rode through this ranch dozens of times on his way to the Elkhorn. It is now a part of Theodore Roosevelt National Park.

"It is a very desolate place, high, barren hills, scantly clad with coarse grass, and here and there in sheltered places a few stunted cottonwood trees; "wash-outs" deepening at times into great canyons, and steep cliffs of most curious formation abound everywhere, and it was a marvel to me to see how easily our mustangs scrambled over the frightful ground which we crossed, while trying to get up to the grassy plateaus over which we could gallop. There is very little water, and what there is, is so bitter as to be almost a poison, and nearly undrinkable; it is so alkaline that the very cows milk tastes of it."

To Alice Roosevelt
September 8, 1883

# THEODORE ROOSEVELT NATIONAL PARK

The original Theodore Roosevelt National Memorial Park entrance station.

Theodore Roosevelt had nothing to do with the establishment of Theodore Roosevelt National Park. And yet the park would not exist if Roosevelt had not come to Dakota Territory in 1883 to hunt buffalo and fallen in love with the stark and eerie badlands country. Roosevelt established two ranches in the Dakota badlands—the Maltese Cross a few miles south of Medora and the Elkhorn Ranch 35 miles north along the Little Missouri River.

Roosevelt later said that he would never have become president of the United States had it not been for his time in North Dakota between 1883-87.

Although talk about creating a park to commemorate Roosevelt began soon after his death in 1919, it was not until 1947 that Congress established Theodore Roosevelt National Memorial Park. In 1978, the park's name was changed to Theodore Roosevelt National Park. In the same legislation, 29,920 acres within the park were designated as Theodore Roosevelt Wilderness.

The park is the home to buffalo, elk, deer, pronghorn antelope, prairie dogs, coyotes, bighorn sheep, and a variety of birds, and some of the most beautiful country in America.

Theodore Roosevelt National Park consists of 70,447 acres in three non-contiguous units. The South Unit consists of 46,158 acres. It is bisected on its south end by Interstate 94. The North Unit consists of 24,070 acres located approximately 60 miles north of Medora. The Elkhorn Ranch Site, consisting of 218 acres, is located halfway between the two larger units of the park.

It is accessible by canoe, foot traffic, or automobiles along dirt roads from either side of the Little Missouri River.

It is fitting that a National Park was dedicated to Roosevelt's memory. He was one of the greatest conservationists in U.S. presidential history, and some of his conservation ideas were developed in the Dakota badlands. Roosevelt also played an important role in the development of the National Park System.

> *I wish I were with you out among the sage brush, the great brittle cottonwoods, and the sharply-channeled, barren buttes.*
>
> — THEODORE ROOSEVELT
> TO FREDERIC REMINGTON

The only part of Theodore Roosevelt National Park with which he had a special relationship was the Elkhorn Ranch Site, where he built a cabin in late 1884 and early 1885, grieved for his first wife Alice, and wrote parts of several books. Of course, Roosevelt rode through the South Unit of today's Theodore Roosevelt National Park scores of times on his journeys to and from the Elkhorn.

The park does not include several areas of special importance to Roosevelt. The Maltese Cross Ranch is privately owned, though TR's Maltese cabin is now on permanent display at the park's South Unit visitor center. The Gregor and Lincoln Lang cabin, which served as a hunting headquarters, has disappeared. The site is privately owned. The place where Roosevelt apprehended boat thieves in 1886 is located near but not in the North Unit of Theodore Roosevelt National Park. Wibaux (Mingusville), where Roosevelt punched out a drunken gunslinger in a bar, is 30 miles west of the park.

Theodore Roosevelt National Park is nestled inside the 1.2 million acre Little Missouri National Grassland, a multiple-use district administered by the U.S. Forest Service that mingles public and private ranch land.

## NUMERICAL INDEX

Clay Jenkinson wishes to express his deep gratitude to Wallace Dailey, the curator of the Theodore Roosevelt Collection at Harvard's Houghton Library; to Sharon Kilzer, Krystal Thomas, Grant Carlson, and Stacy Cordery at the Theodore Roosevelt Center at Dickinson State University; to Dr. James Hutson of the Library of Congress; and to Sarah Trandahl of the Lewis and Clark Fort Mandan Foundation.

Introduction – Photographs courtesy a cooperative effort between the Library of Congress and the Theodore Roosevelt Center at Dickinson State University. Hereafter cited as Library of Congress and Theodore Roosevelt Center.

14  Theodore Roosevelt Collection, Harvard College Library (520.13-001)

15  Theodore Roosevelt Collection, Harvard College Library (520.12-002)

16  Library of Congress and Theodore Roosevelt Center

17  Library of Congress (LC-USZ62-44434)

18  Theodore Roosevelt Collection, Harvard College Library (Roosevelt R500.P69a-017)

19  Library of Congress, (LC-USZ62-113665)

20  Theodore Roosevelt Collection, Harvard College Library (MC196-264-4)

21  National Park Service

22  Library of Congress and Theodore Roosevelt Center

23  Library of Congress (LC-USZ62-49351)

24  Theodore Roosevelt Collection, Harvard College Library (Roosevelt R560.6.C71-049)

25  Library of Congress

26  Library of Congress (LC-USZ62-25802)

27  Library of Congress

28  Theodore Roosevelt Center Dickinson State University

29  Theodore Roosevelt Collection, Harvard College Library (520.14-007)

30  Theodore Roosevelt Collection, Harvard College Library (560.14-042)

31  Theodore Roosevelt Collection, Harvard College Library (520.14-003)

32  Theodore Roosevelt Collection, Harvard College Library (560.14-096a)

33  Library of Congress (LC-DIG-stereo-1s02164

34  Theodore Roosevelt Collection, Harvard College Library (Roosevelt R500.P69a-012)

35  State Historical Society of North Dakota (0119-017)

36  State Historical Society of North Dakota (E0433)

37  Montana State Historical Society (981-010)

38  Theodore Roosevelt Collection, Harvard College Library (560.14-101)

39  Theodore Roosevelt Center Dickinson State University
   National Park Service

41  Theodore Roosevelt Collection, Harvard College Library (520.14-002)

42  Courtesy Gary Lippart

43  Theodore Roosevelt Collection, Harvard College Library (Roosevelt R500.P69a-011)

44  Library of Congress and Theodore Roosevelt Center

45  Library of Congress and Theodore Roosevelt Center

46  Theodore Roosevelt Collection, Harvard College Library

47  Montana State Historical Society (981-402)

48  Theodore Roosevelt Collection, Harvard College Library (560.14-098)

49  Theodore Roosevelt Center, Dickinson, North Dakota

50  Montana State Historical Society

51  Google Images

52  Theodore Roosevelt Collection, Harvard College Library (560.14-075)

53  Theodore Roosevelt Collection, Harvard College Library (520.14-008)

54  State Historical Society of North Dakota (2003-p-10-0093a)

55  State Historical Society of North Dakota (00042-087)

56  State Historical Society of North Dakota (00042-078)

57  State Historical Society (1972.215.1 & 2)

58  Herman Hagedorn, *Roosevelt in the Badlands*

59  State Historical Society of North Dakota (July 22, 1886 Vol. 3 No. 23 Badlands Cowboy); inset: North Dakota State Historical Society.

60  Montana State Historical Society

61  Montana State Historical Society (981-510)

62  Theodore Roosevelt Collection, Harvard College Library (560.14-001e)

63  Theodore Roosevelt Collection, Harvard College Library (560.14-001d)

64  Library of Congress and Theodore Roosevelt Center

65  Theodore Roosevelt Collection, Harvard College Library (520.14-001); inset: Courtesy Gary Lippart

66  Library of Congress and Theodore Roosevelt Center

67  Library of Congress (LC-USZ4-11866)

68  Theodore Roosevelt Collection, Harvard College Library (520.14-004)

69  Theodore Roosevelt Collection, Harvard College Library (560.14-001b)

70  Theodore Roosevelt Collection, Harvard College Library (560.14-092)

71  Library of Congress (LC-DIG-stereo-1s01952)

72  Library of Congress and Theodore Roosevelt Center

73  Theodore Roosevelt Collection, Harvard College Library (560.14-001h)

74  Library of Congress and Theodore Roosevelt Center

75  Library of Congress (LC-DIG-stereo-1s02333)

76  Library of Congress and Theodore Roosevelt Center

77  Library of Congress (LC-USZC4-7934); inset: Library of Congress and Theodore Roosevelt Center

78  Library of Congress and Theodore Roosevelt Center

79  Library of Congress (LC-USZ62-66286)

80  Library of Congress and Theodore Roosevelt Center

81  Library of Congress (LC-DIG-stereo-1s01941

82  Library of Congress (LC-USZ62-68295)

83  Theodore Roosevelt Collection, Harvard College Library (Roosevelt R500.R67-033)

84  Library of Congress and Theodore Roosevelt Center

85  Library of Congress; inset: Library of Congress (LC-USZ62-23055)

86  Library of Congress (LC-USZ62-63967)

87  Theodore Roosevelt Collection, Harvard College Library (520.22-003); inset: Library of Congress and Theodore Roosevelt Center

88  Library of Congress and Theodore Roosevelt Center

89  Jacob Riis

90  Theodore Roosevelt Medora Foundation

91  Theodore Roosevelt Collection, Harvard College Library (560.14-001c); inset: Library of Congress and Theodore Roosevelt Center

92  Theodore Roosevelt Center, Dickinson, North Dakota

93  Theodore Roosevelt Center, Dickinson, North Dakota

94  Library of Congress and Theodore Roosevelt Center

95  Library of Congress (LC-DIG-stereo-1s01931)

96  Library of Congress (LC-USZ62-90051)

97  Clay Jenkinson Private Collection

98  Library of Congress and Theodore Roosevelt Center

99  Library of Congress (LC-USZ62-69318); inset: Library of Congress and Theodore Roosevelt Center

100  Theodore Roosevelt Collection, Harvard College Library (560.3-026)

101  Library of Congress (LC-USZ62-23702)

102  Library of Congress and Theodore Roosevelt Center

103  Theodore Roosevelt Center, Dickinson, North Dakota

104  Library of Congress and Theodore Roosevelt Center

105  Library of Congress (LC-DIG-stereo-1s02355); inset: Library of Congress and Theodore Roosevelt Center

106  Theodore Roosevelt Center, Dickinson, North Dakota

107  Library of Congress (LC-DIG-stereo-1s02033)

108  Library of Congress and Theodore Roosevelt Center

109  Library of Congress (LC-USZ62-55630)

110  Library of Congress and Theodore Roosevelt Center

111  Library of Congress (LC-D4-3646)

112  Library of Congress and Theodore Roosevelt Center

113  Theodore Roosevelt Collection, Harvard College Library (560.51 1903-113)

114  Library of Congress (LC-USZ62-36760)

115  Library of Congress (LC-USZC4-4698)

116  Library of Congress and Theodore Roosevelt Center

117  Library of Congress, (LC-DIG-stereo-1s0286); inset: Library of Congress and Theodore Roosevelt Center

118  Library of Congress and Theodore Roosevelt Center

119  Library of Congress (LC-USZ62-128069)

120  Library of Congress and Theodore Roosevelt Center

121  Library of Congress (LC-DIG-stereo-1s02223)

122  Library of Congress and Theodore Roosevelt Center

123  Library of Congress

124  Library of Congress and Theodore Roosevelt Center

125  National Park Service

126  Library of Congress and Theodore Roosevelt Center

127  Library of Congress (LC-DIG-ppmsc-02647)

128  Theodore Roosevelt Collection, Harvard College Library (560.52 1906-005)

129  Library of Congress (LC-DIG-stereo-1s02149)

130  Library of Congress (LC-DIG-ggbain-06238)

131  Library of Congress (LC-USZ62-51782)

132  Library of Congress (LC-USZ62-24287)

133  Library of Congress (LC-USZ62-51405)

134  Library of Congress (LC-USZ62-78261)

135  Library of Congress (LC-B2 -2521-7)

136  Library of Congress and Theodore Roosevelt Center

137  National Park Service

138  Library of Congress and Theodore Roosevelt Center

139  Library of Congress and Theodore Roosevelt Center

140  Library of Congress and Theodore Roosevelt Center

141  Montana State Historical Society (981-568)

142  Theodore Roosevelt Center, Dickinson, North Dakota

143  Library of Congress (LC-DIG-ggbain-11815)

144  Library of Congress and Theodore Roosevelt Center

145  Library of Congress (LC-DIG-ggbain-11285); inset: Library of Congress and Theodore Roosevelt Center

146  Library of Congress and Theodore Roosevelt Center

147  Library of Congress (LC-USZ62-998)

148  Library of Congress (LC-USZ62-86991)

149  Library of Congress

150  National Park Service

151  National Park Service
   Library of Congress and Theodore Roosevelt Center

135  Library of Congress (LC-USZ62-998)
   Library of Congress (LC-USZ62-86991)

137  Library of Congress
   National Park Service

139  National Park Service